MATT & TOM OLDFIELD

ULTIMATE FOOTBALL HEROES

DONNARUMMA

FROM THE PLAYGROUND TO THE PITCH

DINO

First published in the UK in 2026 by Dino Books,
an imprint of Bonnier Books UK,
5th Floor, HYLO, 105 Bunhill Row,
London, EC1Y 8LZ
www.bonnierbooks.co.uk

X @UFHbooks
X @footieheroesbks
www.heroesfootball.com
www.bonnierbooks.co.uk

Paperback ISBN: 978 1 78946 931 8
E-book ISBN: 978 1 78946 971 4

The authorised representative in the EEA is
Bonnier Books UK (Ireland) Limited.
Registered office address: Block B, The Crescent Building
Northwood, Santry
Dublin 9, D09 C6X8, Ireland
compliance@bonnierbooks.ie

A CIP catalogue record for this book is available from the British Library

Typeset by Envy Design Ltd
Printed and bound by CPI (UK) Ltd, Croydon CRO 4YY

DONNARUMMA

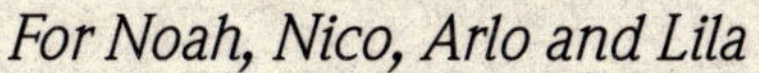

For Noah, Nico, Arlo and Lila

Matt Oldfield is a children's author focusing on the wonderful world of football. His other books include *Unbelievable Football* (winner of the 2020 Children's Sports Book of the Year) and the *Johnny Ball: Football Genius* series. In association with his writing, Matt also delivers writing workshops in schools.

Cover illustration by Dan Leydon.
To learn more about Dan, visit danleydon.com
To purchase his artwork visit etsy.com/shop/footynews
Or just follow him on X @danleydon

TABLE OF CONTENTS

ACKNOWLEDGEMENTS

First of all I'd like to thank everyone at Bonnier Books for supporting me and for running the ever-expanding UFH ship so smoothly. Writing stories for the next generation of football fans is both an honour and a pleasure. Thanks also to my agent, Nick Walters, for helping to keep my dream job going, year after year.

Next up, an extra big cheer for all the teachers, booksellers and librarians who have championed these books, and, of course, for the readers. The success of this series is truly down to you.

Okay, onto friends and family. I wouldn't be writing this series if it wasn't for my brother Tom. I owe him so much and I'm very grateful for his belief in me as an author. I'm also very grateful to the rest of my family, especially Mel, Noah, Nico, and of course Mum and Dad. To my parents, I owe my biggest passions: football and books. They're a real inspiration for everything I do.

CHAPTER 1

ITALY'S SPOT-KICK KING

11 July 2021, Wembley Stadium

After a short wait in the tunnel, it was Italy who led the way out onto the pitch. Their captain Giorgio Chiellini was at the front of the line, smiling confidently, closely followed by his team's giant goalkeeper, Gianluigi 'Gigio' Donnarumma, with a look of total focus on his face. He strolled straight past the glittering trophy without even glancing at it.

'Not now,' Gigio told himself. All that glory could wait; first, they had to win the game, the Euro 2020 final at Wembley!

Around the stadium, sixty thousand England

fans cheered, but the much smaller group of Italy supporters did their best to make as much noise as possible too.

Forza Italia! Forza Italia!

What an amazing atmosphere, and what an exciting sporting event! For Gigio, it would be his first major tournament final since taking over as Italy's first-choice keeper, replacing his childhood hero, the brilliant Gigi Buffon. Back in 2006, Buffon had helped lead his country to World Cup glory; was Gigio about to follow in his footsteps and bring another big trophy back home?

During the early stages of Euro 2020, Italy hadn't really needed their incredible keeper to make too many saves, but since the tense knockout rounds started, Gigio's influence had been growing with every game.

In the quarter-final game against Belgium, he had kept out killer strikes from Kevin De Bruyne and Romelu Lukaku, and in the semi-final match against Spain, he'd been Italy's shoot-out hero. Now, could Gigio save the day again in the biggest game of all?

Forza Italia! Forza Italia!

But before Gigio had even touched the ball, England were already winning. One moment, Italy had a corner at the other end of the pitch, and the next, Luke Shaw was launching a quick counterattack. Uh-oh. Three slick passes later, Shaw was racing in at the back post to slam a shot into the bottom corner. *1–0!*

Woah, what had just happened? At first, Gigio just kneeled there like a statue, arms outstretched, frozen in shock, but that wasn't going to help Italy to fight back. So, pulling himself up to his feet, he began encouraging his teammates.

'Come on, there's still plenty of time to turn this around!' Gigio called out, clapping his big hands together.

He hoped that if he stayed calm and confident, then that feeling would spread to the rest of the Italy players. So when crosses came into his box, Gigio came out to claim them, and when shots flew towards him, he caught them safely in his gloves.

Hurraaaaaaaay!

And when Federico Chiesa dribbled forward and

fired a shot just wide of the England goal, Gigio didn't moan and groan in his goal. Instead, he clapped and shouted, 'That's it – much better!'

At half-time, the score was still 1–0 to England, but after the break and more positive messages from their manager Roberto Mancini, Italy came out fighting even harder in the second half. Lorenzo Insigne curled a free kick just over the bar, then Chiesa forced the England keeper Jordan Pickford to make an excellent diving save, and finally, in the 67th minute, Leonardo Bonucci bundled the ball into the net. *1–1!*

'Yesssssssssssss!' Gigio yelled, throwing both arms up in the air.

Italy were back in the game, but could they now go on and score another? No – not before the final whistle blew, and not in extra-time either. But thanks to some brave goalkeeping from Gigio, they didn't concede a goal either. So, with the score at 1–1 – time for… PENALTIES!

Again! Yes, for the second time in five days, Italy were about to take part in a tense penalty shoot-out, and they were relying on Gigio to save the day…

'Come on, I can do this,' he kept muttering to himself, walking over to the goal, while going over plans he'd made with his coaches for facing each and every England player.

Unfortunately, there was no stopping the first two spot-kicks from Harry Kane and Harry Maguire, but when Andrea Belotti missed for Italy, Gigio knew that he had to stop England from scoring their next one.

So as Marcus Rashford stepped up, he stood tall and still for as long as he possibly could, forcing the striker to make the first move. Eventually, he dived down low to his left, and the shot from Rashford… hit the post! *MISSED!*

Instead of cheering loudly, Gigio just calmly held one fist up in the air, as if to say, 'Don't worry, I'm here to save the day.'

When Jadon Sancho went next for England, Gigio repeated the same trick of watching and waiting until the last second, before diving down to the left… and it worked again! This time, he had guessed the right way, and so with strong hands, he pushed the shot away. *SAVED!*

'Come onnnnnn!' Gigio roared, but he was so focused on trying to save each penalty that he'd totally lost track of the score. Were Italy now winning or drawing in the shoot-out? He had no idea, and so when Jorginho's spot-kick was saved, for a second, Gigio feared that the Euro 2020 final might be over. But it couldn't be, because England's next taker was walking forward: Bukayo Saka.

Right, what should Gigio do now – dive to the left once more, or go the other way this time? In the end, he went for the first option and… it worked again! With firm wrists, he blocked Saka's shot too. *SAVED!*

So, what was the score in the shoot-out now? Still unsure, Gigio just walked to the side of the goal without any celebration, but he looked up to see all of his teammates going wild as they raced towards him…

'Yesssssss, Gigio, you hero!'

'You did it, we've won!'

'Forza Italia! Forza Italia!

Yes, it was all over and Italy were the Euro 2020 winners, thanks to Gigio, their spot-kick king!

After lots of happy hugs and tears, finally it was

glory time, and Italy's incredible keeper had a hat-trick of prizes to collect:

First, the Player of the Tournament award,

Then his gold winners' medal,

And finally, the most important one of all: the Euro 2020 trophy!

Up on the stage, Italy's captain Giorgio stood in the middle of all his amazing teammates, and raised the silver cup high into the London sky.

Hurraaaaaaaay!

Campeones, Campeones, Olé! Olé! Olé!

Standing at the back, with both arms above his head, Gigio was determined to enjoy every single, magical moment. Because after years of hard work, the football-mad kid from Castellammare di Stabia had just become a European Champion.

CHAPTER TWO

CASTELLAMMARE'S NEXT GREAT KEEPER

'Antonio, where are you?' Enrico Alfano asked impatiently while waiting in the hallway for his nephew to appear. Then, glancing down at his watch, he added, 'We're going to be late for practice unless we leave RIGHT NOW!'

Enrico was one of the football coaches at the Asd Club Napoli in Castellammare di Stabia, a small coastal town in southern Italy. It sat 30 kilometres south of Naples and less than 10 kilometres away from Pompeii, an ancient town that had famously been destroyed when the nearby volcano, Mount Vesuvius, erupted in 79 AD.

In modern times, however, Castellammare had become famous for a different reason: football. The area had been developing a strong reputation for producing talented young players, so strong that Club Napoli had even started calling themselves 'School of Champions'! Other than Fabio Quagliarella, a promising forward who was now starring for Torino, Castellammare was best known for one position in particular: goalkeepers.

When he was younger, Enrico had been a keeper himself, but now he was helping coach Ernesto Ferraro to train up the next generation:

Gennaro Iezzo, who was already playing for Serie A club Cagliari, Antonio Mirante, who had recently joined the Juventus academy...

...And now, his own nephew Antonio!

The boy's parents, Alfonso and Marinella, weren't really massive football fans, and so instead it was Uncle Enrico who had first got Antonio into the game, and who often still took him along to training...

'Coming!' a young voice called out from somewhere in the house. Finally!

Then, a few seconds later, another, even younger voice called out, like a quieter, squeakier echo.

'Coming!'

Even in his hurry to get to practice, Enrico couldn't help but smile. Gigio! You see, Antonio wasn't the only eager young keeper in Castellammare; he wasn't even the only one in his own family. No, his brother Gianluigi, or 'Gigio' as everyone called him, was still only four years old, but he was already determined to follow in his goalie gloveprints. After months of watching his big brother in action, he had decided that now, it was his turn to play ball too.

'I'm ready!' Gigio announced, entering the hallway with a big grin on his little face, and two massive gloves on his little hands.

'Good to see you!' Enrico grinned back. 'Now, where is that big brother of yours…?'

After Antonio appeared at last, the three of them made their way down to the Club Napoli training ground as quickly as they could. Once they arrived, Antonio ran off to find his friends in the Under-14s, but Gigio? Well, he was still too young to join a proper team, so Uncle Enrico had decided he would start training him up himself.

'Come on, then, Gigio – let's see if you can save any of my shots!' he challenged his youngest nephew who looked so tiny standing there in the middle of the goal.

BANG!... GOAL!

But even though they were practising on a painful dirt pitch, rather than soft grass, brave Gigio didn't care; he dived all over the place, trying to stop every ball.

BANG!... GOAL!

And even though the big ball kept slipping through his little hands and landing in the net, determined Gigio didn't give up; he kept going, until eventually…

BANG!... SAVED!

'Well done, Gigio – what a stop!' Enrico cheered encouragingly as his shot was blocked.

He could teach his little nephew all of the technical skills later, just as he'd done with Antonio, but for now, the main thing was that Gigio was already showing two of the most important qualities you needed to become a great keeper:

*1) **Fearlessness** to throw yourself to the floor,*
again and again and again,

and

*2) **Resilience** to keep bouncing back up for more,*
no matter what!

And it wasn't long before young Gigio was showing a third key quality:

*3) **Confidence** in your own ability*

When a scout from top Italian club AC Milan came to Castellammare to invite Antonio to sign for their academy, he then turned to his younger brother and jokingly said, 'So, are you a keeper too?'

'Yes!' Gigio replied with real passion, and without a single doubt in his five-year-old, football-mad mind. Because why on earth would he want to play in any other position?

CHAPTER THREE

BRILLIANT BUFFON:
THE OTHER GIANLUIGI AND THE WONDERFUL 2006 WORLD CUP

At the age of seven, Gigio was finally allowed to start playing proper matches for Club Napoli, and he loved almost everything about it:

The teamwork and team spirit,

The danger and the drama…

…And of course, all the chances for him to be a shot-stopping hero!

'Yessssss, thanks Gigio – you saved the day again!'

The only part he really didn't like? Losing. But luckily, with him in goal, that didn't happen very often to his team!

As well playing lots of football, Gigio also found himself watching lots of football, especially during the summer of 2006, because it was time for the next… FIFA World Cup!

The World Cup was a big moment for all fans, young *and* old, but for Gigio it was set to be extra-special because it was the first one where he was old enough to get involved. Plus, with the tournament taking place in nearby Germany, he would be able to watch every game on TV, and hopefully cheer his country on to victory!

Along with Brazil, Germany, England and France, Italy were one of the top five favourites to lift the World Cup trophy, and their squad was packed with superstars.

In attack, they had skilful playmakers like Francesco Totti and Alessandro Del Piero, as well as sharpshooters like Luca Toni and Filippo Inzaghi.

In midfield, they had the passing of Andrea Pirlo, combined with the passion of Gennaro Gattuso,

In defence, they had Alessandro Nesta and Fabio Cannavaro, two of the best centre-backs in the world…

And in goal? Well, in Gigio's humble opinion, Italy had the number one of all number ones: Gianluigi Buffon.

What a spectacular shot-stopper Buffon was, and what a hero for the other, younger Gianluigi to look up to; not only were they both keepers, but they even shared the same first name!

Despite all that talent, however, Italy had only reached the Round of 16 at the 2002 World Cup, and then at Euro 2004, they'd failed to even get past the group stage. So, could they come back stronger in 2006, and lift the World Cup trophy for a fourth time? That was the aim, and back home in Castellammare di Stabia, Gigio was behind them all the way.

Italia! Italia! Italia!

With wins over Ghana and the Czech Republic, Italy successfully finished top of Group E. Part one of the plan: completed! Now, onto the knockout rounds…

Italia! Italia! Italia!

On a Monday afternoon after school, an anxious Gigio sat glued to the TV screen as Italy struggled against Australia in the Round of 16.

'No way, ref – that's never a red card!' he yelled angrily when defender Marco Materazzi was sent off early in the second half. Uh-oh, how were Italy going to win now, with only 10 men on the pitch? For the next 40 minutes, they defended magnificently, and then, just when it looked like the game going all the way to extra time, something amazing happened.

From out wide, Italy's left-back Fabio Grosso dribbled into the Australia box, past one defender and then another. But as he twisted away from the second tackle, Grosso suddenly fell to the grass.

'PENALTY!' Gigio screamed at the TV screen, along with millions of other Italy fans around the world, and this time, they got their wish.

With seconds to go, up stepped Totti, who… slammed his shot past the Australia keeper. *1–0 to Italy!*

'YESSSSSS!' Gigio cheered with joy and relief, jumping up and down on the family sofa. 'We're going to win the World Cup!'

At the time, that sounded like a very bold claim, but in the quarter-finals, Italy cruised past Andriy

Shevchenko's Ukraine, thanks to an early goal from right-back Gianluca Zambrotta, and then two more from Toni.

'See, I told you!' Gigio boasted to his friends at school. 'We're going to win the World Cup!'

In the semi-finals, however, Italy were in for a much tougher test against the hosts and three-time World Champions: Germany, who had magician Michael Ballack in midfield, plus the tournament's most in-form striker, Miroslav Klose.

'Bring it on!' Gigio declared confidently. 'We've got Buffon in goal, and he'll save every shot!'

At the time, that sounded like another bold claim, but he turned out to be correct. That night in Dortmund, Buffon was at his brilliant best:

Tipping a fierce strike from Bernd Schneider over the bar,

Racing out to close down Klose before he could shoot,

Blocking a surprise shot from Lukas Podolski…

…And then leaping high to push another one away from goal.

Hurray, what a hero! Italy's only problem was that at the other end, they were finding it hard to score themselves. First Alberto Gilardino hit the post, then Zambrotta hit the crossbar, but at last, late in extra time, Grosso got the goal they needed, curling the ball into the far corner of the net. *1–0 to Italy!*

'YESSSSSSSS!' Gigio cheered louder than ever, and moments later he was celebrating again, as Del Piero scored a second. 'We're going to win the World Cup!'

Now, for the final, the only team standing in Italy's way was France, but in Zinedine Zidane, they had one of the best players on the planet, and he was in fantastic form. The 2006 World Cup final was set to be the last match of his incredible international career...

Gigio wasn't worried, though. 'He won't beat Buffon!' he announced, as if it was a fact.

But this time, he was wrong. In only the seventh minute of the match, Zidane stepped up to the penalty spot and... chipped the ball over Buffon's diving body, and in off the crossbar. *1–0 to France!*

'There's no way that crossed the goal-line!' Gigio complained to himself at home, but it was no use. Italy were losing, and they would just have to fight back.

Italia! Italia! Italia!

Just 12 minutes later, they were level again. From a Pirlo corner, up jumped Materazzi to power a header past the France keeper. *1–1 – game on!*

'Come on, come on…' Gigio muttered to himself as the minutes ticked by and the tension built.

First Toni's header hit the bar…

…And then at the other end, Buffon tipped Zidane's header over the bar.

So, which team was going to win the World Cup – Italy or France? As the match moved into extra time, the action was even and end-to-end, but everything changed in an instant. Before Gigio really knew what was going on, the referee was pulling out a red card and waving it at… Zidane!

But what had he done wrong? As the replays soon showed, France's captain had turned around and headbutted Materazzi in the chest! Wow, what a moment of pure madness, and what an opportunity for Italy to go on and win the World Cup…

In the end, the final went all the way to a penalty shoot-out, and Gigio could hardly bear to watch. But fortunately for him and Italy, their first four takers all scored, while David Trezeguet hit the bar for France. So, as Grosso walked forward from the halfway line, he had the chance to win the World Cup for his country…

'Come on, come on…' Gigio muttered to himself, peeking nervously through his hands.

After what felt like ages, Grosso stepped up to the spot, and with a powerful curl of his left foot, he… sent the keeper the wrong way! It was all over and Italy were the new World Champions!

'YESSSSSSSSSSSSS!' Gigio roared, and he raced around his living room in wild excitement. What a moment, and what an achievement! Who knew, maybe one day if he kept practising and improving, he might get the chance to win a trophy for his country too…

Italy's heroes of 2006 had just inspired this young, football-mad boy to dream bigger than ever: Totti, Pirlo, Cannavaro, Grosso, and of course best of all, the brilliant Buffon.

CHAPTER FOUR

AC MILAN ALL THE WAY – PART 1

Still buzzing from Italy's wonderful World Cup win, Gigio began working harder than ever on the training pitch at Club Napoli. Every day after school, he couldn't wait to get there and get in goal, so that he could keep improving his game.

Sometimes, Gigio still practised with his uncle Enrico, but mostly, he now trained with the experienced Ernesto Ferraro, the best mentor any young keeper could ask for. Whatever advice his amazing coach gave him, Gigio listened carefully and tried to learn as quickly as possible.

Kicking,

Catching,

Throwing,

One v ones,

Saving shots…

'That's it – great work, Gigio!'

Thanks to all their hours on the training pitch together, he was getting better and better at every aspect of goalkeeping.

And if his practice ever got cancelled because of bad weather? Gigio would get so upset that he cried!

'Don't worry, you'll be able to train again tomorrow,' his mum Marinella always told him, but for Gigio, in the moment, tomorrow felt like forever away.

One day, a newspaper reporter came to the Club Napoli training ground to speak to Ferraro about his incredible record of developing top goalkeepers: Iezzo, Mirante, Antonio Donnarumma… But in fact, Ferraro was most interested in talking about his latest young superstar!

'People will think I'm crazy,' he told the reporter, 'but Gigio will be the best of all. He's got what it takes to become a great keeper.'

Really? The boy was still only eight years old! How could Ferraro be so sure about him?

'Because when I show him something, I don't need to show him again,' the coach explained. 'He already understands. He loves to train too. Gigio never tires.'

Wow! Gigio was delighted to receive such high praise from his coach, and he was determined to prove him right. The older Gigio got, the taller he grew, and the more football he got to play. Because soon, he wasn't just representing his own age group, the Class of 1999; Club Napoli were also asking him to go in goal for the year above, the Class of 1998.

Two matches every weekend? Sure, why not! With his footballing passion, Gigio just wanted to play as many games as possible. That was the best way for him to improve his skills and become the great keeper Ferraro believed he could be, both for Italy… and for AC Milan!

Gigio already knew that was the team he wanted to play for when he was older, but why them, rather than his nearest club Napoli, or the reigning Serie A champions Inter Milan? Well, it certainly helped that his big brother Antonio was already at AC Milan, and regularly sent home parcels full of club kit for Gigio to proudly wear – but that wasn't the only reason.

It was a hard thing for Gigio to explain, but from the very start of his football journey, AC Milan had always been his favourite team. Back in 2005, he had cried tears of sorrow when they collapsed from 3–0 up to lose on penalties against Liverpool in the Champions League final. Two years later, he had cried tears of joy as he watched AC Milan make it back to the final again, where this time they beat Liverpool 2–1 to be crowned European Champions.

What a night, and what a club! Gigio loved everything about AC Milan: the red and black stripes on their home shirt, their famous old San Siro Stadium, and of course all their world-class superstars:

Captain and legendary defender Paolo Maldini,

Top scorer and star striker Andriy Shevchenko,

Nesta, Gattuso, Pirlo and Inzaghi, four of Italy's greatest heroes from their 2006 World Cup triumph,

Magical Brazilian playmaker Kaká, whose face appeared on the clock in Gigio's football-covered bedroom…

…And giant Brazilian goalkeeper Dida, whose poster he proudly displayed on his wall, alongside the brilliant Buffon.

What a team! So when Gigio got the chance to wear his own football kit to training, he always went for an AC Milan shirt.

When he was given new exercise books at school, he always decorated them with the AC Milan badge.

And if one day Gigio got lucky enough to choose which of Italy's top teams he could play for? Well, that would be an easy decision; it was AC Milan all the way!

CHAPTER FIVE

AC MILAN ALL THE WAY – PART 2

By the time Gigio turned 10 years old, word was already spreading far beyond Castellammare di Stabia about Club Napoli's new hot-shot keeper.

Catching? *Tick!* Gigio was big and brave enough to claim every cross that came into his box.

Shot-stopping? *Tick!* With his athletic dives and long, stretching arms, it was almost impossible to score past him.

Kicking? *Tick!* His powerful boot could fire the ball all the way from one end of the pitch to the other, but he also had the accuracy to launch dangerous attacks with clever long passes to his teammates.

'Nice one, Gigio – you're the best!'

Thanks to all his tireless training with Ferraro, Club Napoli's next great keeper was now so talented that he was being asked to play *THREE* matches every weekend: first, for his Class of 1999 team, and then also for the older Classes of 1998 and 1997 too.

'Bring it on!' Gigio told himself as he prepared for kick-off. He loved testing himself against bigger, better and smarter strikers; it was all part of his learning process.

And he was now so tall that when his mum Marinella went along to watch him play for his actual age group, she always brought along Gigio's birth certificate, just in case one of the parents on the other team tried to complain, which they often did.

'Come on – there's no way that keeper is only 10 years old!' they'd argue angrily once Club Napoli were winning against them. 'Just look at the size of him – he fills the whole goal!'

'Look, here you go,' Marinella would reply calmly, showing them her son's birth certificate to shut them up.

'Oh right, okay… err, sorry about that… He's just so good!'

Yes, Gigio really was special, and his coaches at Club Napoli, Ferraro and Angelo Panariello, had known it since the very beginning. They knew that he had everything he needed to become a top keeper – the technical skills – but also the strong character, the courage and confidence, the determination and dedication. They also knew, sadly, that it was only a matter of time before their great Gigio moved on to a bigger and better football team, just like his brother Antonio had done.

But where would Gigio go?

To his nearest club Napoli? No.

To one of the many other Serie A clubs chasing him, including Fiorentina, Roma and Udinese? No.

To Juventus, where he could follow in the footsteps of his hero, the brilliant Buffon? No.

To the reigning Serie A champions, Inter Milan? Hmmm… maybe!

At the age of 13, Gigio travelled up to their academy for a trial, where he even got to work with their legendary goalkeeping coach Luciano Castellini. Gigio loved every minute of it, and he was very close to signing a contract, but there was one thing stopping him: the club he really wanted to play for, most of all, were Inter's local rivals, AC Milan!

Was that a good idea, though, after what had happened to his brother? Following seven frustrating years at the club, Antonio had recently taken the big decision to move on and join Genoa, but Gigio wasn't going to let anything get in the way of his ultimate football dream. Despite his brother's disappointment, he still wanted to go to AC Milan and become the new Dida, their next Number 1!

There was just one problem with Gigio's great plan, however; AC Milan hadn't actually tried to sign him... yet.

Although their scouts had come to Club Napoli many times to watch him play, so far they hadn't made Gigio a firm contract offer. But that all changed once AC Milan's chief scout Mauro Bianchessi heard about Gigio's trial at Inter. Suddenly, he knew that he needed to act fast.

Walking straight into Adriano Galliani's office, Bianchessi told the AC Milan vice-chairman, 'Boss – there's this kid who I really believe is going to be the goalkeeper of the future. He's the strongest I've ever seen, but if we don't do something quickly, he's going to join Inter instead.'

Inter? No way – they couldn't let that something like that happen! Suddenly, the AC Milan vice-chairman was paying full attention. 'Okay, so what's his name?' he asked.

'Gigio Donnarumma.'

Galliani smiled. 'Ah – Antonio's younger brother?'

Bianchessi nodded.

'Good – I know the boy's family well, so that should help,' Galliani said. 'Right, what are we waiting for? Let's go and get this deal done!'

In no time at all, the AC Milan vice-chairman was sitting down at a table with the Donnarummas again, trying to persuade their second son to join the club.

Luckily for Galliani, he didn't have to try very hard at all. As Gigio listened carefully, a big grin spread across his face; he couldn't believe what he was hearing. Wow, his favourite team was now desperate to sign him? Well then, his mind was made up – it was AC Milan all the way!

THE BIG MOVE TO MILAN

When it was finally time for Gigio to make the long journey north from Castellammare to Milan, there were lots of tearful goodbyes.

'See you soon, we'll miss you!' his grandfather cried as Gigio departed.

'My darling boy! Don't forget to call us every week,' his mum sobbed when she hugged Gigio at the train station. 'Be safe and make sure you behave yourself!'

'Don't worry, Mamma – I'll be good, and I'll be fine,' Gigio reassured her with a calm and confident smile. 'I'm off to follow my football dream!'

And he wasn't the only one; there were three other

promising young players – two from Castellammare and one from Naples – travelling on the same train with Gigio, and then on to the AC Milan academy. How exciting! As the four of them set off on their big adventure together, they turned up their favourite Neapolitan tunes extra loud, and sang and danced all journey long.

'Milan, here we come!' they cheered.

By the time they reached their destination, however, that early buzz had faded and the doubts and fears were beginning to creep in. The boys were about to arrive at a big new football club in a big new city, and what if they didn't like it? What if it didn't feel like home? For Gigio, still only 14 years old, this was his first time alone, away from Castellammare and his family, and so he looked around the train station nervously, unsure of what to expect.

Luckily for Gigio and his new friends, one of the AC Milan youth coaches was there waiting to meet them, and then take them to Vismara, the home of the club's academy. There, they were given a guided tour of all the facilities: the changing rooms, the medical rooms, the gym, and of course, the perfect training pitches.

'Wow!' Gigio thought to himself, walking around with wide, eager eyes. 'Compared to Club Napoli, this place is a palace – I can't wait to get started!'

During those first few weeks at the AC Milan academy, Gigio found that the days flew by really fast, with lots of football and fun times with his new teammates. But each night when he went to bed, and each morning when he woke up, Gigio felt very sad and lonely because he really missed his friends and family back in Castellammare.

'Mamma, I want to come home!' he cried on the phone one night, but as much as Martinella wanted to see her son, she knew that she couldn't let him give up on his dream now.

'Gigio, my boy, you need to keep going and give it a bit more time,' she told him. 'I know it's hard right now, but be strong. You'll get used to it, I promise.'

His mum was right. A few weeks later, Gigio began to find his big move to Milan a lot easier. Off the pitch, he settled into academy life, playing video games with a group of teammates every evening, once they'd finished all their training and schoolwork. And on the pitch, Gigio was already on a fast-track to the AC Milan first team!

After starting out in the Under-16s, Gigio played so well that he was soon called up to the Under-18s, and he also got to appear in the 2014–15 Coppa Italia Primavera, the biggest national competition for Under-20 teams. There was Gigio, in the same AC Milan starting line-up as Italian youth internationals like defender Davide Calabria, midfielder Manuel Locatelli, and forward Patrick Cutrone – not bad, considering Gigio was still only 15 years old!

'Mate, you'll be training with the first team in no time,' Manuel predicted confidently.

And he was right. During his second season at the club, Gigio carried on playing matches for the AC Milan junior teams, but in practice, he got to spend more and more of his time working with the seniors.

Hurray, what an exciting opportunity! There were already four goalkeepers in the first-team squad – Michael Agazzi, Stefano Gori, club legend Christian

Abbiati, and Diego López, a new signing from Real Madrid – but at such a young age, Gigio wasn't really looking for game-time yet. For now, what he wanted to do was learn from the very best.

Although Kaká, the last of Gigio's great childhood heroes, had left AC Milan that summer, they still had hugely experienced pros like Michael Essien and Nigel de Jong, plus plenty of awesome attackers:

Japanese playmaker Keisuke Honda,

Italian wing wizard Stephan El Shaarawy,

French forward Jérémy Ménez…

…And best of all, superstar Spanish striker Fernando Torres.

Bring it on! So what if Gigio was still only 15? Taking up his position in goal at the Milanello training ground, he showed no signs of nerves or fear. He loved testing himself against top players in practice, and he was determined to prove that he belonged there at football's highest level.

BANG!… SAVED!

BANG!… SAVED!

Great work, Gigio!

His shot-stopping skills soon caught the attention of the new AC Milan manager, Filippo Inzaghi. Yes, the striker who Gigio had grown up watching as a young boy, who had helped Italy win the 2006 World Cup, was now his coach – incredible!

While Diego was definitely Inzaghi's first-choice keeper, he also liked to have two back-up options on the subs bench for every Serie A game. Usually, those spots were filled by Christian and Stefano, but everything changed in February 2015, when Diego got sent off against Empoli.

Oh dear – AC Milan's Number 1 would now be suspended for one match, at home against Cesena, so who would go in goal? In the end, it was Christian who moved into the starting line-up, but that left a free spot on the subs bench. Would Inzaghi give it to Michael? Instead, the AC Milan manager decided to call up his youngest keeper…

CHAPTER SEVEN

THE BEST BIRTHDAY PRESENT EVER!

'G DONNARUMMA'

Yes, three days before he turned 16, Gigio saw his name appear in the AC Milan matchday squad for the very first time – talk about the best birthday present ever!

'This is MASSIVE!' Gigio told himself, his whole body already buzzing with adrenaline.

He had shared the great news with his family straight away, and now he couldn't wait for his big day to begin. As his team's third-choice keeper, he knew that he had pretty much zero chance of actually playing in the match against Cesena, but for now, that really didn't matter. What mattered was that he was about to achieve so many of his childhood dreams all at once:

Travelling to the stadium on the first-team bus,

Warming up on the San Siro pitch,

Walking out of the tunnel to the roar of the crowd…

…And having his very own official AC Milan shirt number!

It was a day full of so many exciting moments and so many emotions for young Gigio, but which number had he chosen to wear with pride? Well, the classic keeper numbers, 1 and 13, had already been taken by other AC Milan players, and so had most of the other shirts up to 35. But in Italian football, players were allowed to choose any number, all the way up to…

'99!' Gigio decided happily. After all, 1999 was the year he'd been born, and so his childhood team at Club Napoli had been called the Class of 99.

Wearing his new number proudly on his team tracksuit, Gigio took his seat on the AC Milan subs bench, next to his academy friends Ivan De Santis and Gian Filippo Felicioli, as well as famous, experienced players like Alex, Michael Essien, and Keisuke Honda. Amazing!

'Milan! Milan!'

When the game kicked off, Gigio couldn't help cheering along with all of the other supporters in the packed stadium, but this time, for the first time, he was there at the San Siro as a footballer, as well as a fan. It was a moment and a feeling that he would never, ever forget.

It turned out to be a great day for AC Milan, as well as for Gigio. In goal, Christian kept calm and kept a clean sheet. Meanwhile, in attack, Giacomo Bonaventura scored with a brilliant low strike, and then super sub Giampaolo Pazzini made it 2–0 in the very last minute.

'Milan! Milan!'

'I LOVED it!' Gigio told his friends and family afterwards. 'And hopefully, I'll get to do it again soon…'

When Diego returned from his suspension, Gigio

dropped out of the AC Milan matchday squad, but luckily it wasn't for long. By mid-April, he had jumped above Stefano in Inzaghi's keeper list and back onto the subs bench!

And this time, Gigio got to stay there for the rest of the 2014–15 Serie A season:

For home games against Sampdoria and Genoa,

For the massive Milan derby against Inter…

…And also for away trips to Udinese and then to Napoli!

For Gigio, that game was also a great chance to go back home and visit his friends, family and old football coaches in Castellammare, who were all so proud of his progress at AC Milan.

'Congratulations my boy, you're already so close to becoming a star!' everyone told him, from his grandfather to Ernesto Ferraro at Club Napoli. 'Do you think you'll get to make your debut before the season ends?'

Gigio could only smile and shrug; he had no idea, really, but it was a debut that soon looked unlikely, now that he was about to set off on another fantastic football adventure: to Bulgaria, to represent his country at the Under-17 Euros!

'Italia! Italia! Italia!'

Gigio had been looking forward to the tournament for months, ever since the manager Bruno Tedino had first named his 18-man squad. Although he was the youngest player on the trip, Gigio would be surrounded by friends. He already knew five of his teammates from the AC Milan academy – Manuel and Patrick, plus defenders Andrea Malberti and Andrés Llamas, and midfielder Mattia El Hilali – and he also knew other players like striker Gianluca Scamacca from the Italy Under-15s and 16s.

'Come on, we're going to win that trophy!' Gigio told his teammates when they arrived at their base camp in Bulgaria.

'Of course we are,' Manuel agreed, 'but can you please stop playing your Neapolitan music every minute of every day?'

'Hey, you love my tunes really!'

'No Gigio, I really don't…'

For all the fun they had together away from the

pitch, however, the Italy Under-17s were fully focused once the football started. Despite being drawn in the tournament's 'Group of Death', along with England, the Netherlands, and the Republic of Ireland, Gigio and his teammates were feeling confident that they could finish in the top two and make it through to the Euro quarter-finals.

First up: England. On a soaking wet night in Burgas, both teams struggled to play their best football, but sadly for Italy, it was their opponents who scored the only goal of the game. Early in the second half, England's sub striker Marcus Edwards managed to fire a shot past Gigio's desperate dive, and that was that – one game, one defeat for Italy.

'Never mind, boys – we've still got two more group matches to go!' Andrés their captain said, trying to lift the team spirit while they trudged off the pitch, drenched and disappointed.

Next up: Ireland. It was a must-win match for Italy now and they got the job done, thanks to goals from Simone Lo Faso and Simone Mazzocchi, plus some super saves from Gigio.

Those three points lifted Italy into second place going into their final group game against the Netherlands, which meant they only needed a draw to go through. When Patrick scored in the sixth minute, it looked like they would go on and win, but unfortunately, there was nothing Gigio could do to keep out defender Federico Giraudo's freak own goal.

Noooooooooo!

Oh well – a draw was still enough; when the final whistle blew, Italy were through to the Euro quarter-finals!

'Yesssssss!' Gigio cheered, throwing his arms up in the air, and then around his happy teammates.

There wasn't much time to celebrate, though, because three days later, Italy would be taking on the tournament favourites, France…

'Come onnnnn!' Gigio cried out with passion before kick-off, but sadly his team got off to the worst possible start. France striker Odsonne Édouard flicked in their first goal after only five minutes, and after that, there was only going to be one winner. If it wasn't for

Gigio's shot-stopping skills, the final score could have been much wider than 3–0.

At the end, the Italian players slumped to the floor in despair and defeat, but for Gigio, there was at least one small positive to take from his team's early exit: he would now be back at AC Milan in time for the last two matches of the Serie A season…

For the first against Torino, Gigio sat watching on the subs bench again, but ahead of the last game away at Atalanta, there was lots of talk that Inzaghi might select him to start. Really?! Well, AC Milan had nothing left to play for that season, so with the pressure off, why not let their 16-year-old keeper make his club debut?

In the days leading up to the game, Gigio tried not to get too excited, and that turned out to be a good thing because in the end, Inzaghi decided to stick with Christian in goal instead.

Never mind – Gigio knew that his time would come at AC Milan, and it turned out to be sooner than even he had expected…

CHAPTER EIGHT

THE FUTURE OF MILAN AND ITALIAN FOOTBALL

During the summer of 2015, there were more changes at AC Milan. After the team finished 10th at the end of his first season in charge, Inzaghi was sacked and replaced by another Serie A legend called Siniša Mihajlović.

Straight away, Mihajlović set about trying to improve the team by signing quality players in every key position:

A new star striker? Yes, Colombian Carlos Bacca came in from Spanish club Sevilla…

A new central midfielder? Yes, Andrea Bertolacci arrived from rivals Roma…

A new centre-back? Yes, young Italian international Alessio Romagnoli joined the club, again from Roma…

A new keeper? No! The new AC Milan manager decided that he already had enough good options in goal. In fact, Mihajlović had actually let two of his keepers leave: Stefano to Bari, and then Michael on loan to Middlesbrough. That left only three for him to choose from:

Diego,

Christian…

…And Gigio!

Diego was expected to be AC Milan's Number 1 again, but for Gigio, a new manager meant a new chance to impress, and so he was more motivated than ever to perform well during pre-season training.

BANG!… SAVED!

BANG!… SAVED!

Great work, Gigio!

Mihajlović was successfully impressed. During their pre-season tour to China, AC Milan played the mighty Real Madrid in an International Champions Cup match, and in the 72nd minute, Mihajlović decided to change his keeper. Off went Diego, and on came…

Gigio! Wow, what an amazing opportunity, and he was determined to take it with both of his big hands. As he took his position in goal, the score was still 0–0, and with Gigio's help, it stayed that way until the final whistle. So, what now? The answer was… a penalty shoot-out!

Diving low to his left, Gigio managed to save one spot-kick from Toni Kroos, but with the score tied at 9–9, it was time for the keepers to step up. Kiko Castilla went first for Real Madrid and scored, but Gigio's spot-kick was… saved – and so Real Madrid were the winners!

Noooo! Gigio turned and walked away with his head in his hands, but actually, there were reasons to feel positive. Because despite his penalty miss, Mihajlović was now even more impressed by him. Hmmm, he thought – maybe this kid was ready to be more than just a third-choice keeper, after all…

When the 2015–16 Serie A season started, Gigio

stayed sat on the subs bench for the first two months, but in October, when AC Milan went three games without a win, the fans started calling for a keeper switch.

Diego had conceded four goals against Napoli, and then in their draw against Torino, he had been beaten at his near post. Could Gigio do better a job? AC Milan were about to find out because Mihajlović had decided that it was time to make a change. The day before their next match against Sassuolo, he called his young keeper into his office and asked him a simple question:

'Are you scared to play tomorrow?'

In a flash, Gigio replied with a firm and confident, 'No'.

'Good,' his manager said with a smile, 'because you're going to make your AC Milan debut.'

Wow, finally, his dream was about to come true – what an incredible feeling! With his heart pounding in his chest, Gigio thanked Mihajlović and returned to training, but as soon as the session ended, he called his parents to tell them.

'Mamma, Papà – guess what? I'm going to play tomorrow against Sassuolo!'

'My boy, that's brilliant news!' Alfonso said, once their screams of celebration had died down. 'And it's a 2 p.m. kick-off?'

'Yes, but don't worry if you can't—' Gigio began to explain, but his mum quickly butted in.

'We'll be there, son – we wouldn't miss it for the world!'

Having sat on the AC Milan bench for months, Gigio already knew the matchday routine very well, but now that he was actually part of the starting line-up, everything felt different:

Travelling to the stadium on the first-team bus,

Warming up on the San Siro pitch…

…And especially walking out of the tunnel to the roar of the crowd.

Because now, the 35,000 AC Milan supporters in the stadium really were cheering for *him*, their exciting new stopper, who at the age of 16 years and 242 days, was about to become the youngest keeper ever to start a Serie A match!

'Okay – time to shine,' Gigio told himself, taking up his position between the goalposts. For the next 90 minutes, he needed to stay calm and stay focused, ready for any shots that came his way…

From wide on the right wing, Sassuolo's danger man Domenico Berardi looked to cut inside and curl the ball goalwards, but his shot was blocked by AC Milan's left-back Luca Antonelli. The rebound, however, fell to midfielder Karim Laribi, who hit a fierce strike… straight at Gigio! When he caught the ball with his big hands, he breathed a big sigh of relief. Phew, first save completed!

At the other end, however, the Sassuolo keeper Andrea Consigli wasn't so lucky. In the 30th minute, he was sent off for fouling Carlos, who then got back up and scored from the penalty spot. *1–0 to AC Milan!*

It was so far so good for Gigio on his Serie A debut, but early in the second half, disaster struck. As Berardi ran up to take a long-range free kick, Gigio decided to take a small step to his left – BAD IDEA! By the time he moved his feet back across to his right, it was too late. The ball was already flying past his outstretched arm and into the net. *1–1!*

Down on his knees, Gigio threw his arms up in despair. Nooooo – AC Milan weren't winning anymore, and it felt like it was all his fault! Yes, it was a fantastic free kick, but surely he should have saved it? Oh well, at least there were still 40 minutes of the match to go…

'Milan! Milan!'

Giacomo's cross was cleared off the Sassuolo goal-line…

Then Luca sliced a great chance wide…

But finally, with less than 10 minutes left, AC Milan managed to score again. Giacomo's corner was flicked on at the front post, and there was super sub Luiz Adriano on the edge of the six-yard box, to head the ball home. *2–1!*

'YESSSSSSSSSS!' Gigio yelled, punching the air with a mix of passion and relief. Phew – AC Milan were going to win the game after all!

When the final whistle blew, Gigio walked around the pitch with a big smile on his face, sharing happy hugs and high-fives with all of his teammates. Hurray, his AC Milan debut had ended with a victory, but the big question now was: had he done enough to stay in the starting line-up?

After the match, Diego praised Gigio to the media, describing him as the future of Milan and Italian football.

Wow, how kind of his rival keeper! And his manager Mihajlović also praised Gigio in his post-match interview. With three reliable goalkeepers to rotate between, they were going to see if Donnarumma would play against Chievo. There was sufficient time between then and Wednesday.

When Wednesday came around, Gigio was back in goal for AC Milan, and he was there to stay.

CHAPTER NINE

THE HIGHS AND LOWS OF BEING MILAN'S NEW NUMBER ONE

While Gigio still wore '99' on the back of his shirt, it soon became clear that really he was AC Milan's new Number 1. So what if he was still only 16? His manager Mihajlović trusted him, and his teammates did too.

'Well done, Gigio,' they congratulated him after his first clean sheet helped them beat Chievo 1–0. 'We knew you'd save the day!'

But while it was an amazing honour to play in goal for a world-famous club like AC Milan, it was also a lot of pressure for such a young keeper to cope with. In the position Gigio played, he was always going to make mistakes, and what then? How would he react – and how would the fans react?

AC Milan had achieved three wins and a draw in Gigio's first four games in goal, but next up was a seriously tricky away trip to Juventus. Not only would it be a battle between two of Italy's top teams, but it would also be a battle between two of Italy's top keepers: young Gigio versus his idol, the brilliant Buffon! So, who would win: the student or the master?

Gigio was certainly the busier of the two keepers, but at half-time, it was still 0–0 thanks to a series of super saves.

'Great work, Gigio!' his centre-back Alessio cheered, giving him a big high-five.

Early in the second half, he pushed away another powerful strike from Paul Pogba, but unfortunately there was nothing he could do to stop Paulo Dybala from scoring in the 65th minute. *1–0 to Juventus!*

'Noooooooooo!' Gigio groaned as he turned and watched the ball land in his net.

After that, AC Milan did their best to fight back, but at the other end, Buffon simply refused to be beaten. But despite the disappointing defeat, they were still seventh in the Serie A table, and Gigio had clearly impressed his hero with his great performance.

Buffon praised Gigio as a top goalkeeper to the journalists later that season. He also praised Gigio's ability to handle the media pressure incredibly well considering he was only 16 years old.

Wow, thanks Gigi! Gigio would treasure those kind words forever, but he knew that he had to stay focused and keep working hard, day after day, week after week. Otherwise, the mistakes would start to creep in, and he couldn't let that happen.

For Gigio and his teammates, every match was important, of course, but the one that mattered most was definitely the Milan derby against their local rivals Inter, who also played at the San Siro Stadium. Gigio had been on the bench for the first derby of the season, which Inter won 1–0, but now that he was AC Milan's Number 1, he couldn't wait for the second derby to come around. He counted down the days on his calendar leading up to 31 January 2016, determined and ready to make a difference.

While Gigio had experienced the Milan derby atmosphere before, both as a fan and a sub, it was even more electric out on the pitch. The stands were a sea of red and black – the colours of AC – and the roar of the crowd was mightier than ever.

Milan! Milan! Milan!

'Keep your concentration, just keep your concentration…' Gigio told himself again and again, while he waited for Inter's first attack on goal.

When that arrived, Gigio threw his body down in a flash to block Marcelo Brozović's shot, and then leapt up quickly to dive on the loose ball. Okay, he was in the game now…

In the 33rd minute, Alex gave AC Milan the lead with a powerful header, and while watching from the edge of his penalty area, Gigio threw his arms up in the air and then turned and pumped his fists passionately at the fans behind his goal.

The derby wasn't over and done yet, though. The

AC Milan players still had plenty of work to do, and particularly their athletic young keeper…

When the ball rolled loose on the left side of his box, Gigio rushed off his line at top speed and got there just in time to flick it away from Ivan Perišić. *Phew!*

When striker Mauro Icardi ran through on goal, Gigio stopped his first shot with a dive and then got back up to make it a double save.

Hurraaaaaaaay!

It just wasn't Inter's night. Moments after Icardi hit the post from the penalty spot, AC Milan went up the other end and scored two more goals, through Carlos and M'Baye Niang. *3–0!*

Throwing his arms out wide, Gigio turned and looked up at the fans again with a massive grin on his face. What a night, and what a feeling!

The more games Gigio played for AC Milan, the more confident he felt, both on and off the pitch. At the beginning, he had been very quiet and shy in the dressing room, but now that he'd got to know the senior players better, he felt comfortable to be himself:

a young guy who loved to laugh and have fun. Gigio even started sitting at the front of the team bus, just so that he could play his favourite Neapolitan tunes loud and proud for everyone to hear.

'Nope, I still don't like your music!' Manuel told him, putting his headphones on.

By the end of the 2015–16 Serie A season, Gigio had played 30 matches for AC Milan, conceding 28 goals and keeping 11 clean sheets. Not bad at all, especially for a 17-year-old! And he still had one big game to go…

The cup final against Juventus. Although Christian had been AC Milan's starting keeper throughout their Coppa Italia run, Mihajlović made the massive decision to put Gigio in goal instead for the final. Bring it on! He couldn't wait for his chance to become a hero.

But in the event, other than one fingertip save – to stop a cross from reaching Mario Mandžukić – and one reaction save – to keep out a deflected shot from Pogba, Gigio didn't really have much to do for the first 90 minutes. AC Milan were the team on top, but unfortunately they failed to take any of their chances. At 0–0, the final was going to extra time…

The AC Milan players were tiring, but Juventus pushed forward on the attack, looking for a winning goal. In the 110th minute, Gigio watched as a cross curled across the box and all the way through to striker Álvaro Morata, who was unmarked at the back post. Uh-oh – danger alert!

Gigio threw himself down on the grass to try to stop the shot, but sadly he was too late; the ball was already skidding past his outstretched arm. *1–0!*

Spinning around on his knees to look in his net, Gigio's heart sank. Nooooo, football could be so cruel sometimes! Ten minutes later, when the final whistle blew, Juventus were the winners, and AC Milan were the losers.

For Gigio, the painful memory of that first cup final would last a long time, but hopefully one day, he would get his revenge…

CHAPTER TEN

A SENIOR ITALY INTERNATIONAL!

After a short summer break, Gigio returned to AC Milan raring to go, and he carried on his fine form straight away. In the very first match of the 2016–17 Serie A season, his team were 3–2 up with seconds to go when Torino were awarded a penalty. Uh-oh – were they about to draw their opening game at home? How disappointing!

But luckily, when Belotti stepped up to take the spot-kick, super Gigio guessed the right way. *SAVED!*

'Come onnnnnn!' he screamed as his relieved teammates rushed over to congratulate him. What a hero moment!

With Diego and Christian both gone, Gigio was now undoubtedly AC Milan's Number 1, even if he did still wear '99' on the back of his shirt. Meanwhile, he had already played a few games for Italy's Under-21s, but in September 2016, he received a surprise first call-up to the senior squad for their friendly matches.

Wow, what an honour! For Gigio, it was a dream come true to be picked for the national team, and also to train with the brilliant Buffon, of course. He couldn't wait to learn as much as he could, working up close with the greatest goalkeeper in the world.

Gigi Buffon was still Italy's captain and first-choice keeper, but before their important 2018 World Cup qualifier against Israel, the *Azzurri* were also playing a friendly match against France at the Stadio San Nicola in Bari. Hmmm – so did that mean that Gigio might get his first taste of game-time? All he could do was try his best, and then hope for the best…

In the end, it was Gigi who started the game in goal for Italy, but at half-time, with his team losing 2–1, the manager Gian Piero Ventura decided to make a triple substitution:

Daniele De Rossi was replaced by Riccardo Montolivo,

Andrea Barzagli was replaced by Daniele Rugani…

…And Gigi Buffon was replaced by… Gigio!

'Good luck!' his goalkeeping hero told Gigio as he got ready to walk out onto the pitch as a senior Italy international for the very first time. 'Stay calm, do what you always do, and have fun out there!'

'Thanks, will do!' Gigio replied with an excited smile. As the second half kicked off, he had already made history. Aged 17 years and 189 days, Gigio was the new youngest goalkeeper to ever play for Italy!

There was no time to stop and think about his achievement, though; Italy's new Number 12 needed to focus on the game in front of him, especially the France attackers threatening his goal…

First, André-Pierre Gignac fired well wide of the target, then so did Antoine Griezmann, but the next long-range effort from Dimitri Payet was a lot more accurate. Right, time to shine! Throwing himself down on the grass, Gigio got his body behind the ball and held onto it tightly. *SAVED!*

Hurraaaaaaaay!

With their young keeper off to a solid start, Italy spent the next 20 minutes pushing forward in search of an equaliser. But just when Gigio was thinking he might be on for a second-half clean sheet, all his good work was undone. In the 81st minute, France's left-back Layvin Kurzawa raced into the box to reach a pass from Pogba, and controlled the ball just before it ran out for a goal kick. What next? Surely the angle was too tight for a shot?

'He's going to cross it from there,' Gigio thought to himself, and so he quickly moved forward off his line a little to try and block the ball as it entered the six-yard box. But at the last second, Kurzawa decided to go for goal instead, lifting a clever chip over Gigio's diving body and into the gap he'd left behind…

'Nooooo!' Gigio groaned, turning to see the ball land in the far corner of his net. *3–1!*

Uh-oh, he'd just been beaten at his near post, something that was never supposed to happen to a keeper, but especially not on their senior international debut!

'Okay, just keep calm and keep doing what you do,' Gigio told himself, hurling the ball forward for the restart. Hopefully, there was still time for him to make up for his mistake…

In the final moments of the match, France won a free kick in a good shooting position. Up stepped Pogba, who managed to curl the ball through the Italy wall, but when it flew towards the bottom corner, Gigio threw himself across the goal and stopped it with safe hands. *SAVED!*

Hurraaaaaaaay!

Much better! By the final whistle, Gigio was feeling a bit happier about his overall performance. The video replays and learnings could wait until later; for now, he just wanted to walk around the pitch shaking hands, clapping the fans, and enjoying his massive moment.

So, how did it feel to make his senior debut for his country at the age of just 17?

'It's indescribable,' Gigio told the journalists. 'I thank Coach Ventura for this opportunity and my debut. I am really quite emotional about it.'

Four days later, he was back on the bench watching

another Buffon masterclass – Italy went on to win 3–1 away against Israel.

Italia! Italia! Italia!

For now, Gigio was very happy to be his country's back-up keeper, but one day soon, he was determined to achieve his dream of becoming their new Number 1.

CHAPTER ELEVEN

GIGIO SAVES THE DAY!

23 December 2016, Jassim Bin Hamad Stadium, Qatar

Back at AC Milan, it turned out to be another season, another trophy battle with Juventus. This time, however, instead of the Coppa Italia, the trophy up for grabs was the Supercoppa Italiana, and their battle was taking place in Qatar, just two days before Christmas. Ooooh – a win would be a perfect present…

'Come onnnn, we've gotta beat them this time!' Gigio roared, hungry for sweet revenge.

Under another new manager, Vincenzo Montella,

AC Milan had made a very promising start to the 2016–17 Serie A season. With only two league defeats since September, they were up to third place in the table, behind Roma and the leaders: Juventus!

But thanks to a goal from Manuel and some great saves from Gigio, AC Milan had managed to beat Juventus 1–0 at the San Siro back in October – so could they win again, a long way away from home?

Midway through the first half, their chances didn't look good. Gigio made a brilliant reaction save to block Stefano Sturaro's shot, but from the resulting corner-kick, Giorgio Chiellini scored with an unstoppable volley. *1–0 to Juventus!*

Was it going to be the same sad story all over again for AC Milan? Possibly not – as half-time approached, they attacked the Juventus goal again and again until eventually, the equaliser arrived. From wide on the right wing, Suso curled a dangerous cross into the box and in raced Giacomo to beat Buffon with a beautiful flick header. *1–1!*

'Yesssssssssss!' Gigio screamed loudly from the edge of his penalty area, pumping both fists with passion. It was game on, with all to play for in the second half...

First, Alessio hit the bar for AC Milan with a glancing header, then at the other end, Gigio had to almost fly through the air like Superman to tip Sami Khedira's swerving strike past the post. *SAVED!*

'Great work, Gigio!' Alessio clapped and cheered.

Next, Paulo Dybala fired a shot just wide, and then in the final seconds, Buffon somehow kept out a header from Carlos. How on earth was it still 1–1?! Maybe someone would finally score a winner during 30 more minutes of extra time...

Or maybe not – Italy's top two keepers both simply refused to be beaten again. So there was only one thing for it: the 2016 Supercoppa Italiana would have to be settled by a penalty shoot-out!

While Montella talked to AC Milan's first five takers, Gigio tried to stay calm by going through his penalty-saving plans in his head. Together with the goalkeeping coaches, he had prepared for this moment, working out which players were likely to step up for Juventus, and where they usually placed their spot-kicks: high, low, left or right. But in the big moment, with the pressure on, would their homework pay off? It was time to find out.

Gigio vs Gigi – only one of them could be the trophy-winning hero, but which incredible Italian keeper would it be?

Ooooooooooooooooohhhhhhh… goal!

Despite Gigio's best attempts to guess which way he'd go, Claudio Marchisio managed to send him the wrong way and score. Never mind, Gigio moved straight on to his tactics for Juventus' next taker, Mandžukić…

Waiting on his goal line, Gigio stood tall and still for as long as he possibly could, forcing the Croatian striker to make the first move. Eventually, he dived down low to his left, and the shot from Mandžukić… crashed off the crossbar. *MISSED!*

'Come onnnn!' Gigio cheered, clenching one fist with calm focus. But if AC Milan were going to win the shoot-out and lift the trophy, he still had lots more work to do…

Gonzalo Higuaín stepped up next for Juventus…

and blasted the ball down the middle, just past Gigio's outstretched leg. *GOAL!*

'Argggh, so close!' he muttered to himself in disappointment.

Then Khedira sent Gigio the wrong way with a perfect penalty. *GOAL!*

After eight spot-kicks, the shoot-out was tied at 3–3 – talk about a tense atmosphere! The pressure was really on now because the next team to miss would probably lose the match. Gigio, however, was thinking more positively as he took up his position in goal again. The way he saw it, the next keeper to save a penalty would probably win the trophy…

'I can do this, I can do this,' Gigio kept muttering to himself while Dybala made the long walk forward for Juventus.

After a stuttering run-up, the Argentinian tried to curl a shot into the side of the net… but Gigio had guessed the right way, and with a strong left arm, he batted the ball away. *SAVED!*

Hurraaaaaaaay!

The AC Milan supporters celebrated, and so did

some of the players, but Gigio, their hero who had probably just saved the day, didn't even smile. He walked to the side of the goal because he knew that the match wasn't yet over and won. Milan's fifth and final taker still needed to step up and score…

That was young midfielder Mario Pašalić… who confidently fired a shot into the top corner. Now it really *was* all over – AC Milan had just won the 2016 Supercoppa Italiana!

Milan! Milan! Milan!

And now their superstar keeper was ready for the wild celebrations to begin. He had saved the day for his favourite team and he was the hero of the shoot-out!

'YESSSSSS, GIGIO!'

One amazing minute, he was at the bottom of a big happy, sweaty team bundle, and the next, Gigio was up on the stage, standing tall in the back row, as club captains Riccardo Montolivo and Ignazio Abate stepped forward together to collect the Supercoppa trophy.

3… 2… 1…

Hurraaaaaaaay!

Campeones, Campeones, Olé! Olé! Olé!

With a stretch of his long arms, Gigio reached forward over the heads of his teammates to touch the trophy, his first for AC Milan. The first, he hoped, of many.

CHAPTER TWELVE

YOUNG ITALIANS AT THE EUROS

After the highs of lifting the Supercoppa, sadly AC Milan faded away a little in the second half of the 2016–17 season. Juventus bounced back to beat them in the Coppa Italia quarter-finals, and in Serie A, Milan slipped down from third to sixth spot, which earned them a place in the Europa League, rather than the Champions League.

For Gigio, it had still been a very solid second season – all 38 league games played, 45 goals conceded, with 12 clean sheets – and it wasn't quite over yet. Before his summer holidays began, he was heading off to Poland to play for his country, but not for the senior team this time. Instead, he would be one of the young Italians competing at the Under-21 Euros!

'Let's go win that trophy!' Gigio told Manuel with confidence while they travelled from Milan together.

They were two of the youngest players in a very strong Italy squad that included lots of Serie A stars of the present and future:

Daniele Rugani, who was seen as Juventus's next great defender,

Lorenzo Pellegrino, a midfield maestro who was running the show for Sassuolo,

Domenico Berardi, the skilful forward who had scored a free kick against Gigio back on his AC Milan debut…

…And on the wings, the two Federicos, Chiesa and Bernardeschi, who were already firing together for Fiorentina.

What a talented young team! No wonder Gigio was predicting such big things for them at the tournament in Poland. To reach the semi-finals and beyond, however, Italy would need to finish top of a very tough group, featuring Germany, Denmark and the Czech Republic.

Oof, there would definitely be no easy games at the Under-21 Euros, but Gigio believed in his teammates, and whenever they needed him, he would be there in goal, ready to rescue them.

In Italy's first game against Denmark, Gigio didn't have very much saving to do. In front of him, the defence stood strong, and in attack, Lorenzo scored an amazing overhead-kick, before Andrea Petagna secured the victory with a late second strike.

Three points, two goals, and a clean sheet for Gigio – what a perfect start!

Italy's next match against the Czech Republic, however, turned into a nightmare. Midway through the first half, Gigio conceded his first goal at the Euros, and he wasn't happy about it. Michal Trávník's low shot wasn't that powerful but as Gigio dived across the grass, the ball whizzed just past his outstretched fingertips and into the bottom corner.

'Arghhh, too slow!' Gigio told himself angrily. 'I've got to get down quicker than that!'

Never mind, time to move on… With 20 minutes to go, Italy finally equalised, thanks to a diving header from Domenico – but now what? Should they go for a win, or hold on for the draw? Knowing that they still had Germany to play, Italy chose the first option, but they were soon punished

for that. First, Marek Havlík poked a shot into Gigio's bottom corner, and then Czech centre-back Michael Lüftner surprised everyone by scoring an absolute screamer from 30 yards. *3–1!*

What? How? As he got back up to his feet, Gigio couldn't believe what had just happened. Before he knew it, the final whistle had blown, and Italy had lost. Noooooo! That disappointing defeat was going to make it difficult for them to top the group now, but if they beat Germany in their last game, then they could still make it through to the semi-finals…

Come onnnnnnnnn!

Italia! Italia! Italia!

With their future at the Euros under threat, Italy's players were more motivated than ever. They raced around the pitch fighting hard for every ball, and in the 30th minute, their high pressing paid off.

On the edge of the Germany box, Lorenzo slid in to poke the ball away from Mahmoud Dahoud and into the path of Federico Bernardeschi, who calmly slid a shot through the keeper's legs. *1–0 to Italy!*

'Yesssssssssssss!' Gigio yelled from afar, throwing both arms high above his head.

Right – now it was *his* time to shine! After letting in three goals against the Czech Republic, Gigio was determined to perform better and be the hero in the big game against Germany. But other than intercepting Serge Gnabry's cross to Davie Selke early in the second half, he didn't actually have very much to do. The Italy defenders were doing a brilliant job, and if they ever escaped, Germany's attackers kept missing the target.

'Nearly there now,' Gigio thought to himself as he watched another shot fly wide.

But when the final whistle blew, the Italy players hardly celebrated their win at all, because they didn't yet know the result in the other match between Denmark and the Czech Republic. Eventually the news came in – hurray, Denmark had won, which meant Italy had finished top of the group, after all!

'Semi-finals, here we come!' Gigio cheered while their celebrations began.

There, Italy faced another tough test against Spain, who had won all three of their group games. Marco Asensio, Saúl Ñíguez, Héctor Bellerín, Gerard Deulofeu, Kepa Arrizabalaga – their list of superstars went on and on, but Gigio and his teammates were full of belief that they could beat them.

After a very evenly-matched first half, Spain took the lead early in the second thanks to a beautiful strike from Saúl, and when Italy's midfielder Roberto Gagliardini was sent off a few minutes later, it looked like their Euros adventure might be over. But Italy weren't done yet; back they came with Bernardeschi scoring an excellent equaliser. *1–1 – game on!*

'Yesssssssssssss!' Gigio cried out, but Italy's joy didn't last long. Out of nowhere, Saúl scored again with a long-range rocket that flew right into the corner of the net, leaving Gigio with no chance of stopping it.

'Nooooooooooooo!' he groaned, throwing his arms

up in frustration this time. How quickly a football match could change, and how cruel the game could be! Ten minutes later, Saúl completed his hat-trick and confirmed Italy's exit from the Euros.

Despite the unhappy ending, Gigio had still enjoyed the tournament, and he had also learned a lot from the experience. Now, it was time to head back to AC Milan and make a big decision about his football future…

CHAPTER THIRTEEN

FOUR MORE YEARS IN MILAN

Now that the Under-21 Euros tournament was over, it was decision time for Gigio. Was he staying at AC Milan, or moving on?

Back in mid-June 2017, the club had announced some surprising news: Gigio, their young superstar keeper, had rejected their new contract offer.

What? Why? Really? At first, the fans had been shocked, and then absolutely furious.

'Who does Donnarumma think he is?!' they argued. 'We're the club that gave him a chance, and now he's ready to turn his back on us and chase the big money!'

Some AC Milan supporters had even given Gigio a nasty new nickname – 'Dollarumma' – and during Italy's match against Denmark at the Under-21 Euros, fake money had been thrown into his goal.

All that anger and hate was hard to deal with, especially as an 18-year-old, but Gigio tried his best to keep calm and think things through clearly. Despite what other people said, his decision to reject AC Milan's contract offer hadn't just been about money; it had also been about the future of the club, and whether their ambitions matched his.

Gigio wanted to win as many trophies as possible and play in European football's most famous competition, the Champions League, but could he really achieve those aims at AC Milan? As much as he loved his childhood club, Gigio wasn't so sure. It was now four years since they had even qualified for the Champions League…

His agent, Mino Raiola, praised Gigio's skills as he celebrated the 11 clubs who had shown a clear interest in the goalkeeper – Manchester United, Manchester City, Barcelona, Real Madrid, Atletico

Madrid, Bayern Munich, Juventus, Napoli, Liverpool, Paris Saint-Germain and Everton.

That was a lot of options for Gigio to choose from, but eventually, after long discussions with AC Milan, Gigio changed his mind, and a deal was done. With a big new contract, he would be staying at the club for four more years – plus his brother, Antonio, would be joining him there!

'I'm delighted and proud to be at Milan,' Gigio told the media at a special press conference. 'I was born and raised at this club and I never had any doubts about staying in my mind. I'm sorry to the fans who felt betrayed, but I repeat that was not my intention.'

So, would the fans accept Gigio's apology and forgive him? Yes, as long as he kept performing well and saving the day for his team! It was time for him to focus on football again, and his greatest goal: getting AC Milan back into the Champions League…

After a promising start to the 2017–18 season, they ended up finishing in sixth place in Serie A. To make matters even worse, they also lost 4–0 to

Juventus in the Coppa Italia final, with Gigio at fault for three of the goals. Noooo, what a shocker!

Gigio admitted his disappointment to the fans in a post-match video. But he asked his fans to look to the future.

Could AC Milan bounce back and achieve their aims during the 2018–19 season? Yet despite Gigio's 13 Serie A clean sheets, they finished fifth, just one point behind Atalanta and their local rivals, Inter. Argggh – so close to a Champions League spot! But instead, another year in the Europa League lay ahead…

The 2019–20 season was no improvement for AC Milan – despite Gigio winning the Serie A Goalkeeper of the Year award for the first time, his team finished sixth, one place lower than the previous season. Oh dear, instead of moving forwards, they seemed to be going backwards!

Gigio, meanwhile, only had one year left on his AC Milan contract now, which meant one last chance to achieve his Champions League aim…

'Come on, this *has* to be our season!' he urged his

teammates on. Although Gigio was still only 21 years old, he was now one of the club's longest-standing players, and one of the team leaders too.

For the 2020–21 season, the signs looked better for AC Milan. They had a settled manager, Stefano Pioli, and an exciting squad, combining the energy of young stars like Sandro Tonali, Brahim Díaz and Rafael Leão with the experience of Simon Kjær, Hakan Çalhanoğlu, and legendary striker Zlatan Ibrahimović, who had returned to the club for a second spell.

At the grand age of 39, 'Ibra' started the 'season of fire' with two goals to beat Bologna, and then two more to win the derby against their local rivals Inter.

'Forza Milan!' Gigio roared with passion as the whole team ran towards the fans to celebrate the victory.

After 10 games, AC were still unbeaten, and five points clear at the top of the Serie A table. Was this finally going to be their year? Although Gigio dared to dream, he knew that they had to keep taking things one game at a time:

AC Milan 2 Parma 2,

Genoa 2 AC Milan 2…

'Hey, at least we still haven't lost!' Gigio reminded his teammates.

It was Juventus who finally ended their unbeaten run in January 2021, and after that, AC Milan's season suddenly seemed in danger of falling apart. By April, they had slipped all the way down to fifth place – were AC Milan going to let their Champions League chances fade away yet again? But with five games to go, they launched an incredible fightback, inspired by their new captain: Gigio!

AC Milan 2 Benevento 0,

Juventus 0 AC Milan 3,

Torino 0 AC Milan 7!

What a win! Even after a disappointing home draw against Cagliari, AC Milan still found themselves in fourth place, one point ahead of Juventus, with one game left to play: Atalanta away…

Oooof! It was going to a very tough match against the team in third place, but the AC Milan players were determined to finish the season on a high. Just before half-time, left-back Theo Hernández was fouled as he dribbled into the box. Penalty! Up stepped Franck Kessié… who scored. *1–0!*

'Yessss, come onnnnn!' captain Gigio cheered from his goal. 'Keep going, guys!'

When the second half kicked off, Atalanta flew forward on the attack, but Gigio refused to be beaten.

SAVED!

BLOCKED!

WIDE!

Hurraaaaaaaay!

AC Milan were almost there now, and in the final moments of the match, they were even awarded a second penalty for handball. When Franck stepped up to the spot, Gigio turned away, too nervous to watch, but he could tell the result from the wild reaction of his teammates: *GOAL, 2–0!*

'YESSSSSSSSS!' He was so overjoyed that he ran all the way from his own goal to join in the team celebrations. Hurray, they had done it; after seven years of trying, AC Milan were heading back to the Champions League at last!

But would that be enough to persuade Gigio to

stay at the club for another few years? No, despite also being named Serie A Goalkeeper of the Year for a second season in a row, his mind was already made up. All attempts to agree a new contract had failed, so on 26 May 2021, just three days after that last match of the season against Atalanta, Milan's director of football Paolo Maldini confirmed the bad news that the fans had been fearing.

Maldini praised Gigio as a leader and a captain, and also praised him for how much he gave to Milan. They were moving in different directions, but Milan's director wished the goalkeeper the best.

So, where would Gigio go next?

To Juventus to replace his hero Buffon, who had just moved back to Parma?

To Chelsea or Manchester United, who both had money to spend and keeper problems to solve?

All would soon became clear. For now, Gigio needed to switch his focus from club to country because after a year's delay, Euro 2020 was about to begin!

CHAPTER FOURTEEN

EURO 2020 PART 1: KING OF THE CLEAN SHEETS

Gigio couldn't wait for Euro 2020 to kick off. Not only would it be his first major international tournament, but he was also now Italy's Number 1.

After their disappointing defeat to Sweden in the 2018 World Cup play-offs, several of Italy's senior players had retired from international football, including Daniele De Rossi, Andrea Barzagli, and Gigi Buffon. Since then, the national team had been going through a big rebuild, with fresh new players all over the pitch:

Domenico on the right side of the attack,

Manuel and Nicolò Barella in central midfield,

Leonardo Spinazzola at left-back…

…And, of course, Gigio in goal!

At first, Gigio had shared the role with Torino's Salvatore Sirigu, but it didn't take long for the Italy manager Roberto Mancini to make up his mind.

Mancini had declared Donnarumma was the strongest goalkeeper in the world back in January 2021, after two clean sheets in a row. And now, it was time for Gigio to prove his manager right.

Italia! Italia! Italia!

Playing in front of a roaring home crowd at the Stadio Olimpico in Rome, the *Azzurri* came out attacking with style and speed. Lorenzo Insigne curled a shot past the post, Giorgio Chiellini powered a header just over the bar, Ciro Immobile fired straight at the keeper, and then Leonardo's cross struck the arm of a Turkey defender in the box.

'Handball – penalty!' Gigio called out from his goal along with all of his teammates, but the referee shook his head.

When the half-time whistle blew, it was still 0–0, and the Italy players walked off feeling disappointed.

Would they come to regret those wasted chances? No! In the second half, they kept pushing forward until eventually they got their breakthrough.

In midfield, Manuel played a perfect pass through to Nicolò, who spread the ball wide to Domenico on the right wing, who in turn dribbled his way into the box. His cross was meant for Ciro Immobile in the middle, but it deflected off a Turkey defender and flew into the net. *1–0!*

Hurray, they were winning at last! After that, it was all Italy, and with nothing to do, Gigio watched on like the supporters in the crowd.

'Yesssssssss!' he cheered when Ciro smashed home the rebound after Leonardo's strike was saved. *2–0!*

'Yesssssssss!' he cheered again when Lorenzo curled the ball into the bottom corner. *3–0!*

Three goals and another clean sheet – what a confident way to kick off Euro 2020! 'We couldn't have had a better start,' Gigio wrote to the fans after the game. 'Forza Azzurri!'

Next up was a tricky tie against Switzerland, but again, Italy made it look easy. This time, it was

Manuel who got the opening goal after a storming solo run from Domenico, and he scored again early in the second half with a fantastic finish from the edge of the box. *2–0!*

'Wow, we're looking *really* good!' Gigio smiled to himself while celebrating.

Other than a great double save to deny Steven Zuber, Italy's keeper had another quiet game, and with seconds to go, Ciro completed the victory with a fierce strike that dipped into the bottom corner. *3–0 again!*

'2 wins out of 2,' Gigio posted proudly, plus yet another clean sheet, of course. 'Next round!'

With a match to spare, Italy had already qualified for the knockout stage. But still, they really wanted to keep their winning run going in their last group game against Wales. So while Mancini rested stars like Giorgio, Manuel and Ciro, he decided to keep Gigio in goal, just in case.

Midfielder Matteo Pessina gave Italy the lead just before half-time, and with Gigio making himself big to put off Aaron Ramsey and Gareth Bale, they held for another victory, and another clean sheet.

Italy's reward for topping their group was a Round of 16 tie against Austria at Wembley Stadium. So far, they had cruised their way through Euro 2020, but things were about to get a little more nerve-wracking in the knockout rounds.

In the first half, Italy were definitely the better team, but their attackers just couldn't put the ball in the net. Lorenzo and Nicolò both had shots saved by Austria's keeper Daniel Bachmann, and then Ciro's swerving strike clipped the post. *So close!*

'Unlucky, keep going!' Mancini told his players. 'The goal will come!'

But in the second half, Austria raised their game, and in the 65th minute, it looked like Marko Arnautović had given them the lead with a header that looped over Gigio's upstretched arms. But no, after a VAR check, the goal was ruled out for offside. Phew! On the game went, and into extra time…

In the 95th minute, Leonardo controlled the ball on the left and curled a beautiful pass across to substitute Federico Chiesa, who was unmarked on the right side of the box. As a desperate Austria defender charged towards him, Chiesa calmly tapped the ball through his legs, and then smashed a shot into the far corner of the net. *1–0!*

Hurray – Italy were winning at last, and 10 minutes later, Matteo scored a second goal. *2–0* – game over? Not quite – Austria weren't done yet.

Gigio had to dive down at full-stretch to stop a fierce low strike from Louis Schaub, and then before the final whistle, he conceded his first goal of the tournament. Saša Kalajdžić's clever flick header flew through a crowd of defenders and into the net before Gigio could get down and keep it out. *2–1!*

Noooooo! After a record-breaking 1,168 minutes of football, Italy had finally let in a goal. Gigio's run of clean sheets was over, but the main thing was that his team was through to the Euro quarter-finals!

Afterwards, Gigio summed the game up perfectly on social media: though it was a challenge to achieve victory, his team would never give up!

And Italy would need to show lots more of that fighting spirit in their next match against… Belgium! Even with Eden Hazard out injured, the 'Red Devils' still had plenty of attacking talent in their team. With the likes of Kevin De Bruyne, Romelu Lukaku, Youri Tielemans, Jérémy Doku on the pitch, Gigio was expecting to be a busier keeper in this quarter-final, and he was ready for any shots that came his way…

He dived across his goal to stop a blast from De Bruyne with a strong right arm. *SAVED!*

He threw himself down again to push a Lukaku strike away from danger. *SAVED!*

Hurraaaaaaaay!

Great work, Gigio!

Moments later, Italy were up the other end, attacking with intent. After escaping from three Belgium defenders in the crowded box, Nicolò blasted the ball into the bottom corner. *1–0!*

Then, before half-time, Lorenzo added a second, with a sublime curler into the top corner. *2–0!*

Wow, Forza Italia! But just when it looked like they were on their way through to the semis, Belgium got back into the game. Doku was fouled in the penalty area, and up stepped Lukaku, who sent Gigio the wrong way. *2–1!*

It was all set to be a very exciting second half, but fortunately for Italy, Lukaku missed two golden chances to equalise, and slowly the minutes ticked away. As one last header flew over his crossbar, Gigio punched the air with joy. Hurray – Italy were heading through to the Euro 2020 semi-finals!

CHAPTER FIFTEEN

EURO 2020 PART 2: SHOOT-OUT SUPERSTAR

For Gigio, it was like the Under-21s Euros all over again because in the semi-finals, Italy were about to face… Spain!

Although '*La Roja*' still had experienced superstars like Sergio Busquets, Jordi Alba, and Álvaro Morata in their team, they had struggled to win games at the tournament so far. In the group stage, they had drawn with both Sweden and Poland, while in the knockout rounds, they had required extra-time to beat Croatia, and then penalties to beat Switzerland. But in the end, Spain kept finding ways to succeed, and ultimately that was all that really mattered in football.

'Come on, let's go out there and fight until the end!' Gigio told his Italy teammates while they waited in the tunnel at Wembley ahead of the biggest game of their lives. 'And let's make sure that we win!'

Italy vs Spain was a fixture with a long and fierce history. For years, Italy had been the dominant team, but more recently that had changed.

As a nine-year-old, Gigio had watched his country lose to Spain on penalties in the Euro 2008 quarter-finals. And then as a 13-year-old, he had watched the Euro 2012 final, in which Andrés Iniesta and co thrashed his beloved Italy 4–0, a painful experience he would never forget. Four years later, the *Azzurri* had got some revenge, beating Spain 2–0 in the Round of 16, but now, Gigio wanted more…

Forza Italia! Forza Italia!

In a tight first half, the best chance fell to Spain's attacker Dani Olmo, but Gigio got down quickly to block his shot. *SAVED!*

Hurraaaaaaaay!

At the start of the second half, Spain were the team on top, but after catching a cross from Alba, Gigio decided to launch a quick Italy counterattack. He rolled the ball forward to Marco Verratti, who passed it to Lorenzo wide on the left wing, who poked it through for Ciro to chase…

Forza Italia! Forza Italia!

Aymeric Laporte slid in to intercept Lorenzo's pass, but as the ball rolled loose, Federico Chiesa reached it first. And cutting inside onto his right foot, he whipped a perfect shot into the far corner of the net. *1–0!*

Hurraaaaaaaay!

But while Gigio threw his arms up in celebration, he knew that their Euro semi-final was still far from won…

Mikel Oyarzabal missed a golden chance to equalise for Spain, and then Olmo fired a shot just wide. Phew! Could Italy hold on for the victory? No – in the 18th minute, Morata played a one-two with Olmo and calmly placed his shot in the bottom corner, leaving Gigio with no chance. *1–1!*

Game on! Soon, they were heading into extra time, and when neither team scored a winner after 30 more

minutes of tense football action, it was time for…
PENALTIES!

With the pressure on, Italy got off to the worst possible start in the shoot-out. Manuel went first and his spot-kick was saved, but luckily, super Gigio came to the rescue. First, he used his size to pressure Olmo into skying the ball over the bar, and then, after getting his fingertips to Gerard Moreno's strike, Gigio threw himself down to stop Morata's shot. *SAVED!*

Hurraaaaaaaay!

The Italy supporters celebrated, and so did some of the players, but once again, Gigio, their hero who had probably just saved the day, did not even smile. He walked to the side of the goal because he knew that the match wasn't over and won yet. Italy's fifth and final taker still needed to step up and score…

That was Jorginho, who with his trademark skip and a jump… calmly fooled the Spain keeper and found the bottom corner. Okay, now it really was all over, and Gigio could start celebrating. Thanks to his shoot-out save, they were through to the Euro 2020 final!

Forza Italia! Forza Italia!

'Yesssss, Gigio, you hero!' his teammates yelled as they raced over to hug him.

For Italy, it was another wonderful night at Wembley, and they would have an even better night ahead, if they could win the Euro final against… England!

Gigio simply couldn't wait. 'Here we go,' he posted after counting down the days. 'Ready for the final.'

But before he had even touched the ball, England were already winning at Wembley. One moment, Italy had a corner at the other end of the pitch, and the next, England were on the counterattack, with Luke Shaw who was racing in at the back post to slam a shot into the bottom corner. *1–0!*

Woah – what had just happened? At first, Gigio just knelt there like a statue, arms outstretched, frozen in shock, but then, pulling himself up to his feet, he began encouraging his teammates.

'Come on, there's still plenty of time to turn this around!' Gigio called out, clapping his big hands together.

At half-time, the score was still 1–0 to England, but after the break, Italy came out fighting even harder, and in the 67th minute, Leonardo Bonucci finally fired in an equaliser. *1–1!*

'Yessssssssssssss!' Gigio yelled, throwing both arms up in the air.

Italy were back in the game, but could they now go on and score another to win it? Not before the final whistle blew, and not in extra-time either. Oh well, time for… PENALTIES!

For the second time in five days, Italy were about to take part in a tense penalty shoot-out, and they were relying on Gigio to save the day…

Unfortunately, there was no stopping the first two spot-kicks from Harry Kane and Harry Maguire, but when Andrea Belotti missed for Italy, Gigio knew that he had to stop England from scoring their next one.

So when Marcus Rashford stepped up, he stood as tall and still for as long as he possibly could, forcing the striker to make the first move. Eventually, he dived down low to his left, and the shot from Rashford… hit the post! *MISSED!*

By keeping calm and making himself big, Gigio had played a key role in putting the England striker off, and he was about to become even more of an Italy hero.

When Jadon Sancho stepped up next... Gigio dived in the right direction and pushed his shot away. SAVED!

And then when Bukayo Saka ran up to take England's fifth penalty... Gigio threw himself across his goal and blocked his shot too. SAVED AGAIN!

Gigio was so focused on preparing for each penalty that he'd totally lost track of the score, and so he just walked to the side of the goal without any celebration. But as he looked up, he saw all of his teammates going wild as they raced towards him…

'Gigio, you hero!'

It was all over and, thanks to their shoot-out superstar, Italy were the new Champions of Europe!

After lots of wild, emotional celebrations with his teammates, it was finally trophy time, and Gigio was about to have his big hands full. Because as well as his gold winner's medal, he also became the first goalkeeper to ever win the Player of the Tournament award. And finally, there was the most important treasure of all: the Euro 2020 trophy!

Hurraaaaaaaay!

Campeones, Campeones, Olé! Olé! Olé!

When Italy's Wembley celebrations finally ended and the players left the stadium, it was Captain Chiellini who proudly carried the trophy onto the team bus. But when he placed it down on the seat next to him, he heard a voice ask, 'Big Giorgio, will you leave it with me for a couple of minutes?'

What? Why? Looking up, he saw that it was Gigio, their giant keeper and shoot-out hero. 'Oh of course!' the Italy captain replied with a smile. 'Have it – you earned it, my friend!'

CHAPTER SIXTEEN

PICKING... PSG!

The next few days after the Euro 2020 final were
a happy blur for Gigio, as the Italy players returned
home to a hero's welcome. But once the open-top bus
parade through the streets of Rome was over and he
had hugged the trophy for the 200th time, Gigio knew
that he had to move onto to his next challenge, at his
next football club.

Before he officially announced his new home,
however, he wanted to say an emotional goodbye to
his old one:

He wrote a long letter that he posted on social
media, explaining how he joined Milan when he was
a child. After eight years of wearing their shirt with

pride, he had a lot of memories to share with his teammates, his coaches and his fans. He had felt they had all become family.

He wished them every possible success and said how he would always feel connected with this team.

With the hard part done, Gigio was now ready to reveal the new club he was joining on a free transfer: the French champions, PSG!

Gigio was thrilled to join a club as big as Paris Saint-Germain. He was excited by the new challenge ahead of him and was eager to improve. He had a new group of supporters to impress, and he wasn't about to let them down.

Since the arrival of rich new owners Qatar Sports Investments in 2011, PSG had been completely dominating French football. They had lifted the Ligue 1 title seven times in nine years, plus the Coupe de la Ligue and the Coupe de France six times each, and the Trophée des Champions every year. But despite all that success in their own country, there was still one major European trophy missing from the club's cabinet: the Champions League.

Back in 2017, PSG had spent over £350 million on two superstars, Neymar Jr and Kylian Mbappé, but so far, they hadn't managed to win the prize that the club really wanted. After reaching the Champions League final in 2020, they'd lost the big game against Bayern Munich, and so now it was time to try again, with a new manager, Mauricio Pochettino, and new superstar signings in every position:

Gigio in goal,

Achraf Hakimi and Sergio Ramos in defence,

Gini Wijnaldum in midfield…

…And in attack? The one and only Lionel Messi!

Wow, with a front three of Messi, Neymar and Mbappé, and Gigio in goal, how could PSG possibly fail?

Gigio wasn't the only world-class keeper at the club, however. Former Real Madrid stopper Keylor Navas had been their first choice for the last two seasons, and he was still there, and still wearing the Number 1 shirt.

'Okay, no problem,' Gigio told PSG. 'Can I wear 99 instead, like I did in Italy?'

'No, sorry,' the club replied. 'In France, goalkeepers can only wear 1, 16, or 30.'

What? Why? Number 16 already belonged to Sergio Rico, and Lionel wanted 30, so in the end, Ligue 1 allowed Gigio to choose between two extra squad numbers: 40 and 50.

'Fine, I'll take 50,' he decided.

Then, after his tiring summer at Euro 2020, it was time for Gigio to go on a well-deserved holiday with his girlfriend Alessia. But that meant he wasn't fully fit in time for the beginning of the 2021–22 Ligue 1 season, and so Keylor started in goal instead.

'Arghh – I want to be out there playing!' Gigio muttered miserably, watching on from the subs bench while his new team beat Brest and Reims.

At last, in mid-September, Pochettino decided that he was ready to make his PSG debut at the Parc des Princes against Clermont Foot. Hurray! Gigio couldn't wait, and guess what? He kept a clean sheet in a comfortable 4–0 win!

Gigio was off to the perfect start at PSG; surely, he'd be their first choice from now on? But no – four days later in the Champions League, it was Keylor who played against Club Brugge, and Pochettino carried on swapping his keepers for the rest of the season.

But why? Gigio didn't like it, and he didn't understand it. He was the best goalkeeper in the world and in late November, he was awarded the famous Yashin Trophy to prove it. So, why wasn't he playing in every match for PSG?

In Ligue 1, Pochettino often picked Keylor in goal, whereas Gigio was PSG's main man in the Champions League, especially when they made it through to the last 16. There, they faced… the mighty Real Madrid. Oooooh… what an exciting European clash!

PSG were desperate to win the first leg at home at the Parc des Princes, but Real Madrid's keeper, Thibaut Courtois, had the game of his life, saving shot after shot from Kylian, and even a spot-kick from Lionel.

'Noooooooo!' Gigio groaned while watching on from the other end. After dominating the game, a draw would be so disappointing!

But then, deep in injury time, Neymar set up Kylian,

who danced through the Real Madrid defence, and guided the ball into the back of the net at last. *1–0!*

'Come onnnnnnn!' Gigio cried out when the final whistle blew, and pumped his fist at the PSG fans behind his goal. They now had a 1–0 lead to take to the Bernabéu for the second leg – bring it on!

Away in Spain, PSG started the game brilliantly, and after missing a couple of chances and having a goal disallowed, Kylian eventually made it 2–0 on aggregate with a powerful finish just before half-time.

Hurraaaaaaaay!

PSG were now in an excellent position to go through to the Champions League quarter-finals, but with a superstar striker like Karim Benzema up front, Real Madrid were always capable of coming back to win the match…

In the first half, Gigio had made an amazing acrobatic save to keep out a Benzema shot that was curling into the top corner, but in the 60th minute, he unfortunately gifted him a goal. After controlling a back pass from Presnel Kimpembe, Gigio took too long to clear the ball, and Benzema was able to close him down and deflect his kick straight to Vinícius Júnior. Uh-oh – danger alert! The Brazilian pulled the ball back for Benzema, who fired a shot past a desperately diving Gigio. *2–1!*

Nooooooo – what was Gigio thinking? What a silly mistake! Suddenly, Real Madrid were back in the game and as the PSG defence panicked, Benzema punished them.

BANG! His shot flicked off a defender and flew past Gigio's upstretched arm. *2–2!*

BANG! Just seconds later, he pounced on Marquinhos's misplaced pass and poked the ball into the bottom corner. *3–2!*

Three goals in 16 minutes – Benzema had just turned the game around for Real Madrid with an amazing hat-trick, and all Gigio could do was shake his head and throw his water bottle down in despair. From 2–0 up, PSG had collapsed and now they were out of the Champions League. What a nightmare!

That night, Gigio hardly slept at all because he kept thinking about his mistake and what he should have done differently. Arghh – if only he'd just booted the ball away quicker! The next day at training was difficult too, but after that, Gigio knew that he had to move on and put that painful moment behind him.

He admitted on social media that the last two days weren't easy for him, but he was thinking positively and focusing on the here and now, still determined to win the league.

Six weeks later, PSG achieved that aim, clinching the Ligue 1 title with four games to spare. But looking back on the whole of his first season at the club, Gigio was far from satisfied.

'I'll stay at PSG and I'll try to win the Champions League, but I'm here to be the owner of the Number 1 shirt,' he said in an honest interview. 'I have an excellent relationship with Navas, but things certainly have to change.'

CHAPTER SEVENTEEN

THE CHAMPIONS LEAGUE CHALLENGE

For the 2022–23 season, PSG had a new manager, Christophe Galtier, and a new Number 1… Gigio! Well – actually, he had been allowed to wear his favourite '99' instead, but it was clear that he was now the team's first-choice keeper, both in Ligue 1 *and* the Champions League.

Hurray! After his mistake against Real Madrid, Gigio was even more motivated than ever to help PSG achieve their European dream. They flew through the group stage unbeaten, but in the Last 16, they faced another tricky tie, this time against German giants Bayern Munich.

It was a repeat of the 2020 Champions League final, and PSG were out for revenge, but it wasn't going to be easy. Despite selling their star striker Robert Lewandowski to Barcelona, Bayern still had plenty of other dangerous attackers in their squad: Thomas Müller, Serge Gnabry, Jamal Musiala, Sadio Mané, Leroy Sané…

Oh, and they also had a seriously strong defence and one of the best keepers in the world. Manuel Neuer vs Gigio? Brilliant, let the greatest goalie battle begin!

In the first half of the first leg in Paris, Gigio only had one serious save to make, getting down quickly to catch a shot from Joshua Kimmich. But early in the second half, Bayern left-back Alphonso Davies curled a deep cross towards Kingsley Coman, who met it on the volley. The strike wasn't particularly powerful and it flew straight towards Gigio, but somehow he let the ball slip under his body and into the net. *1–0!*

Arghhh! Another error in the Champions League! Gigio was furious with himself, but hopefully

there was still time for his teammates to save
the day…

In the 73rd minute, it looked like Kylian had scored
an equaliser, but no, it was ruled out for offside, and
the same thing happened again in the 81st minute.
So when the final whistle blew, Bayern Munich had a
narrow 1–0 lead to take back
to the Allianz Arena.

'Let's keep our heads held high,' Gigio said
afterwards, trying to stay positive. 'Focus on the
next match.'

With an all-star attack featuring Messi and
Mbappé, surely PSG could score in the second leg?
But no, as hard as they tried, they couldn't get the
goal they needed. Lionel had a big chance blocked
in the six-yard box, and then Vitinha had a shot
cleared off the line by Matthijs de Ligt. *So close!*

PSG just needed to stay calm and keep creating
chances, but in the 60th minute, they gave the ball
away on the edge of their own box. Uh-oh. Müller
passed it to Leon Goretzka, who set up Eric Maxim
Choupo-Moting to score. *2–0 to Bayern!*

Now PSG were in serious trouble, and when Gnabry added a late goal on the counterattack, their early Champions League exit was confirmed.

Not again! PSG went on to win the Ligue 1 title for the second year in a row, but for all his fine performances and clean sheets, Gigio couldn't help thinking back to that Bayern game and the Coman shot he should have saved… Oh well, he thought, there was always next season!

Summer 2022 turned out to be another busy one for PSG. Off the pitch, out went Galtier, and in came former Barcelona manager Luis Enrique. And on the pitch, out went older stars like Lionel, Sergio, Neymar and Marco Verratti, and in came younger players like Manuel Ugarte, Randal Kolo Muani, Bradley Barcola, and Ousmane Dembélé.

So, would the extra pace and energy help PSG to perform better in the Champions League? That was the plan, and with new captain Kylian leading the way, they successfully escaped from a Group of Death featuring Borussia Dortmund, Newcastle United, and Gigio's old club AC Milan.

Phew! So, could they avoid the big boys in the Last 16 this time? Yes – instead their opponents would be… Real Sociedad!

It was still going to be a tough tie against one of the best teams in Spain, but PSG were the clear favourites to win. Kylian and Bardley got the goals in the first leg at home, and then Kylian completed the job with two more away in San Sebastián.

'ALLEZ PSG!' Gigio posted after the match with a special video that ended with an exciting question:

'Next up: Quarter finals?'

The answer turned out to be… Barcelona! The Spanish giants had struggled since losing Lionel Messi in 2021, but now they had a fantastic new front three: Raphinha, Robert Lewandowski, and young superstar Lamine Yamal…

The first leg at the Parc des Princes finished 3–2 to Barcelona, but despite being a goal down, the PSG players arrived in Barcelona for the second leg, feeling confident that they could win it. Even when Raphinha scored an early goal to make it 4–2, they refused to give up. Ousmane pulled one goal back before half-time, and then after the break, PSG were simply unstoppable.

Vitinha fired a low, fizzing shot into the bottom corner. *4–4!*

Ousmane was fouled in the box, and up stepped Kylian to score from the spot. *5–4 to PSG!*

The tie wasn't won yet, though, and Gigio was about to become a busy keeper…

'Come onnnnn!' he cried out after saving a fierce strike from Lewandowski.

'Great work, Gigio!' Marquinhos gave him a high-five after he tipped a Raphinha corner over the crossbar. *SAVED!*

Hurraaaaaaaay!

With 88 minutes of the game played, PSG were nearly there now, and from the corner, Achraf raced away on the counterattack, setting up Kylian to score again. *6–4!*

Game over, what an incredible win – PSG were through to the semi-finals!

Gigio posted photos on social media afterwards of all the players celebrating together in a big, happy huddle. So, after so many seasons of frustration, was this finally going to be their Champions League year?

The signs certainly looked good when PSG were drawn against Borussia Dortmund, rather than Real Madrid or Bayern Munich. They had already played Dortmund twice in the group stage, winning 2–0 at home and then drawing 1–1 away, but if they thought it was going to be as simple in the Champions League semi-finals, they thought wrong.

During the first leg in Germany, Gigio had to make save after save to keep PSG in the game, but there was nothing he could do to stop Niclas Füllkrug's powerful strike from skidding past him and into the net. *GOAL!*

'Offside?' Gigio said hopefully as he got back up, but when he glanced over at the linesperson, he saw that their flag was down.

Early in the second half, Kylian and Achraf both hit the post, but despite lots of chances to equalise, the match finished 1–0 to Dortmund. Clearly, PSG would still have plenty of work to do back home in Paris…

'Oooooooooh… Noooooooooo!' Gigio groaned, feeling all of the emotions of the fans around him, as PSG's attackers missed chance after chance.

So far, he had spent most of the match watching the game going on at the other end of the pitch, but suddenly he was called into action as Dortmund raced forward on the counterattack. When Karim Adeyemi entered the box, he tried to slide a shot into the far corner, but Gigio flew across his goal and stopped it with a strong left hand. *SAVED!*

Hurraaaaaaaay!

Phew – they were still only one goal behind at half-time, but that all changed early in the second half. Just moments after Warren Zaïre-Emery hit the post for PSG, Dortmund went up the other end and Mats Hummels scored a header from a corner. *2–0!*

'Hey, what happened there?!' Gigio called out to his defenders, throwing his arms out wide in anger. 'Who was meant to be marking him?!'

With two goals needed now, PSG went all-out attack, but still the ball just wouldn't go in. Nuno Mendes hit the post, then Kylian and Vitinha both hit the bar. What? How? Gigio couldn't believe what he was seeing. How unlucky could one team get?!

When the final whistle blew, Gigio and his PSG teammates slumped down all over the pitch, crying tears of total despair. Noooooooooo – they had come so close! Another year, another Champions League disappointment; it was Dortmund who were heading through to the final at Wembley, not them.

Gigio admitted his disappointment in a message to the fans the next day, but at the same time, he was already looking ahead to the future.

In the meantime, PSG had another Ligue 1 title to lift, and then another trophy to try and win in the 2024 Coupe de France final against Lyon.

This time, PSG went 2–0 up, thanks to first-half goals from Ousmane and Fabián Ruiz, and although Lyon managed to pull one goal back, Gigio made a series of super saves to inspire his team to victory.

Hurraaaaaaaay!

Campeones, Campeones, Olé! Olé! Olé!

First the Trophée des Champions, then the Ligue 1 title, and now the Coupe de France – despite their

Champions League disappointment, PSG had still ended the season with a hat-trick of club trophies.

Next year, Gigio was aiming to go one better and win the quadruple, but before all that, he had another exciting international tournament to prepare for: Euro 2024! And this time, he would be proudly wearing the armband as the captain of his country…

CHAPTER EIGHTEEN

EURO 2024: CAPTAIN OF HIS COUNTRY

After the excitement of winning Euro 2020, Gigio had pictured himself achieving lots more international success with Italy in the years ahead. So far, however, things hadn't gone according to plan…

The 2021 UEFA Nations League finals? No, rivals Spain had got their revenge, beating Italy 2–1 in the semis.

The 2022 World Cup in Qatar? No, somehow they had failed to even qualify, following a shock 1–0 defeat to North Macedonia in the play-offs.

First 2018, and now 2022 – no Italy for a second World Cup in a row? What a disaster! Of course,

Gigio was far from the only *Azzurri* player to blame for the poor performance, but should he have got down quicker to keep out Aleksandar Trajkovski's swerving long-range strike in the 92nd minute? Yes, probably…

Gigio wrote on social media how disappointed they were, and how he was sure the fans felt the same way. But football was very much like life, he added, as you must always look forward to keep your head in the game. Step by step, he promised, they would bring the national team back to where it deserved to be.

The 2022 Finalissima? No, back at Wembley for another big game, Italy had lost 3–0 against the South American champions, Argentina.

The 2023 UEFA Nations League finals? No, Spain had beaten them in the semis again, this time with a goal in the 88th minute. Arghhh!

But after those four major disappointments, at last there was light at the end of the tunnel because Italy had successfully qualified for… **Euro 2024**. Hurray! And who would be leading the national team as they defended their title in Germany? Yes, Gigio!

He had first worn the armband for Italy way back in October 2021, but now that Giorgio Chiellini and Leonardo Bonucci had both retired from international football, Gigio had officially been named as the next captain of his country.

The armband was a big level of responsibility to carry. He openly spoke of how proud he was to wear it, and how he was eager to bring joy and victory back to the whole country.

Italy's path to the trophy, however, was looking particularly tricky this time. To even get out of their group, they would need to finish above either 2022 World Cup semi-finalists Croatia or 2023 UEFA Nations League winners Spain. That was going to be a massive challenge, especially for a young Italy squad that no longer featured experienced players like Giorgio, Leonardo, Ciro Immobile and Lorenzo Insigne…

'Bring it on!' captain Gigio told his teammates as they prepared for their must-win first match against Albania – but within seconds of kick-off, Italy found themselves 1–0 down. Federico Dimarco's risky throw-in was intercepted inside their own box, and

Nedim Bajrami slammed a shot into the top corner before Gigio could even move.

Noooooo! It was the fastest goal ever scored at the Euros, and the worst possible start for Italy.

'Come on, keep your heads up,' captain Gigio clapped and cheered his team on. 'We can still win this!'

And they did. Italy were soon level, thanks to a header from centre-back Alessandro Bastoni, and in the 16th minute, Nicolò Barella scored a beauty to put them ahead. What a quick turnaround – 2–1, and with some late heroics from their incredible keeper, they managed to hold on for the victory.

'Forza Italia!' Gigio roared at the final whistle, pumping his fists with passion. Phew, they were off to a winning start! Right, onto their next opponents: Spain…

With wingers Lamine Yamal and Nico Williams causing all kinds of problems, Italy were under pressure right from the start, and they could easily have been losing at half-time, if it wasn't for their incredible keeper.

In only the second minute, Pedri's header was sailing into the roof of the net, but up jumped Gigio to push the ball over the bar. *SAVED!*

Morata dribbled into the Italy box, but out rushed Gigio to block his shot with his long legs. *SAVED!*

His PSG teammate Fabián Ruiz hit a powerful long-range strike that zoomed towards the top corner, but super Gigio flew through the air to tip it over. *SAVED!*

Hurraaaaaaaay!

Thanks to Gigio's shot-stopping masterclass, Italy were somehow still in the game, but early in the second half, their goalkeeper was finally beaten. As Williams's cross fizzed through the penalty area, Gigio threw himself down to flick the ball away from danger. Unfortunately, however, his touch deflected the ball against his own defender, Riccardo Calafiori, and into his own net. *1–0 to Spain!*

'Nooooooooooo!' Sprawled out flat in his six-yard box, Gigio's heart sank and he buried his face in the grass. What an unlucky way to let in a goal! But as Italy's captain, he had to get back up and lead by example.

'*Come on, it's not over yet – keep going until the end!*'

As hard as they tried, however, Italy couldn't create an equaliser, and so it finished 1–0 to Spain. Were Italy heading for an early exit at Euro 2024? Not according to their captain, who was still feeling confident.

'We never give up,' Gigio declared. 'We are Italy.'

With a win or draw against Croatia in their last group game, they would almost certainly qualify for the Round of 16, but early in the second half, the ball struck the arm of an Italian defender in the box. Penalty!

Up stepped the Croatia captain Luka Modrić, who aimed for the bottom corner… but down went big Gigio to push the ball firmly away. *SAVED!*

Hurraaaaaaaay!

Italy's joy didn't last long, though. Less than a minute later, the ball was back in their box. Gigio made a great save to stop the first shot from Ante Budimir, but the rebound fell to Modrić, who wasn't going to miss again. *1–0!*

Italy were losing, and their leader was absolutely

furious about it. 'Come onnnnnn, we've got to be better than that!' Gigio screamed at his teammates, jumping up and down with rage.

Once their captain had calmed down, Italy had 40 minutes left to score at least one goal and keep their Euro 2024 dream alive.

'Forza Italia! Forza Italia!'

From a corner, Alessandro powered a header just over the bar, and then in the 87th minute, Gianluca Scamacca was inches away from reaching a cross from Federico Chiesa. *So close!*
Was that it, the end of Italy's Euro 2024 dream? Not quite. In the very last seconds of the match, Riccardo burst forward from defence and slid a pass out to Mattia Zaccagni on the left edge of the box, who calmly whipped a curler into the top corner. *1–1!*

Unbelievable scenes – suddenly Italy, not Croatia, were going through to the Round of 16! Watching the ball land in the net, Gigio was off, sprinting forward to join in the wild team celebrations over by the corner flag.

'Forza Italia! Forza Italia!'

After that amazing comeback moment, Gigio and his teammates were feeling good about their chances against Switzerland in the Round of 16. However, that soon turned out to be over-optimistic, and a match to forget.

Early on, Gigio kept Italy in the game with an excellent save to deny Breel Embolo, but the Switzerland attacks just kept coming. Remo Freuler raced into the box and scored before half-time, and then Rubén Vargas did the same shortly after the break. *2–0!*

This time, there was no late Italy fightback, and so their Euro 2024 dream really was over.

In his post-match interview, captain Gigio didn't hold back. He admitted his frustration, apologising to all Italians. There wasn't much else to say. The team struggled through the whole match, and they were losing their courage.

It was clear that Italy would need to make major improvements if they were going to qualify for the 2026 World Cup. But first, Gigio had another big dream he was determined to achieve, back at PSG…

CHAPTER NINETEEN

WINNING THE CHAMPIONS LEAGUE AT LAST!

Kylian Mbappé was ecstatic to join his dream team, Real Madrid, a move that had been announced just days before the start of Euro 2024.

But while his move marked the end of PSG's superstar era, that didn't mean the French club was giving up on their Champions League ambitions.

Their manager Luis Enrique vowed they would be stronger next season. But how would this be achieved? Well, by building a more balanced, united, hard-working team! PSG already had a talented squad of players, but there were still a few pieces missing from the trophy-winning puzzle.

So, keeper Matvey Safonov came in from Krasnodar to be the back-up for Gigio…

Strong centre-back Willian Pacho arrived from Eintracht Frankfurt to partner Marquinhos at the back…

Energetic box-to-box midfielder João Neves was bought from Benfica to play alongside Vitinha and Fabián Ruiz in the middle…

…And skilful young attacker Désiré Doué signed from Rennes to be Kylian's long-term replacement.

Perfect, now the new PSG were ready to fight for a historic Quadruple!

Together, they lifted trophy number one in January 2025 after Ousmane's late winner in the Trophée des Champions final against Monaco.

'Come onnnnnnn!' Gigio cried out with joy as Willian jumped into his arms. But once the celebrations were over, it was onto the next match and the next trophy…

In early April, PSG were crowned Champions of France yet again, with six Ligue 1 games to spare…

…And then in mid-May, they completed the treble

again by beating Stade Reims 3–0 in the Coupe de France final.

'There's no stopping us this season!' Gigio told Marquinhos with a smile as they walked around the pitch afterwards, clapping the PSG fans. For once, Gigio had been on the bench for the big game, with Matvey starting in goal instead, but he still joined in the celebrations at the Stade de France. That was what being part of a team was all about, and hopefully, their successful season wasn't over yet…

Gigio had posted excitedly on social media in early May about one more important game coming up. Which game was he talking about? The Champions League final, of course!

Yes, after a slow start in the new-look group stage, PSG had found their best form just in time for the knock-out rounds. After thrashing Brest 10–0 on aggregate, they then battled their way past the Premier League leaders Liverpool in the Round of 16. With the scores still tied at 1–1 after two legs, plus extra time, the game went all the way to a penalty shoot-out, where PSG's super-keeper saved the day yet again.

First, Gigio dived to his left to deny Darwin Núñez. *SAVED!*

And then he dived to his right to keep out Curtis Jones. *SAVED!*

Hurraaaaaaaay!

What a hero! Moments later, Désiré stepped up to score the winning spot-kick, but all the PSG players ran to Gigio first – and it was Gigio who got the Player of the Match award.

'MVP! MVP! MVP!' Achraf chanted in the dressing room afterwards, cheekily spraying his keeper with water.

After beating Liverpool, PSG had then knocked out two more English teams:

First Aston Villa in the quarter-finals…

…And then Arsenal in the semis!

In the first leg in London, Ousmane gave PSG an early lead, and after that, it was Gigio's job to protect it. Challenge: accepted!

Gigio stretched out a strong left arm to stop a shot from Gabriel Martinelli. *SAVED!*

Then he threw himself down to tip Leandro Trossard's strike past the post. *SAVED!*

Hurraaaaaaaay!

Clean sheet: completed! At 1–0 – advantage PSG…

In the second leg in Paris, it was a very similar story. This time, it was Fabián who put PSG ahead, and then Gigio's shot-stopping was as good as in the first leg, if not even better!

In a crowded box, he reacted quickly to stop a Martinelli shot from close range. *SAVED!*

Then, despite defenders blocking his view, Gigio somehow managed to dive down and push a powerful low Martin Ødegaard strike round the post. *SAVED!*

'That's astonishing!' cried the commentators on TV.

In the second half, Bukayo Saka cut inside onto his lethal left foot and curled a shot towards the top corner, but Gigio flew through the air to tip the ball over the bar. *SAVED!*

'That's outstanding!' cried the commentators on TV.

Eventually, Saka did score against Gigio, but by then, Achraf had already added another goal for PSG, and so when the final whistle blew, they were through to the Champions League final!

Hurraaaaaaaay!

PSG posted a photo on social media of Gigio throwing both arms up in the air like a true hero.

After the match, even the Arsenal manager was full of praise for him. Mikel Arteta said the goalkeeper was the best player on the pitch. Gigio had made the difference for them in the tie.

So, would Gigio need to make the difference again in the biggest game of them all: the 2025 Champions League final, at the Allianz Arena in Germany? PSG's opponents were Inter Milan, which meant Gigio was lining up against lots of his Italy national teammates: Nicolò, Alessandro, Federico Dimarco, Davide Frattesi…

'Good luck!' they said to each other, 'May the best team win!'

But who would that be? The answer was… PSG! Before Gigio had even made a save, they were already winning the game.

First, Achraf finished off a fast, flowing team move. *1–0!*

Then, in the 20th minute, Désiré fired a shot past

the Inter keeper after a lightning-quick counterattack. *2–0!*

A dream start for PSG, but while Gigio watched and cheered from his goal, he refused to get too carried away. He needed to stay calm and focused, ready for any shots that came his way…

The Inter fightback, however, never arrived. Instead, PSG's perfect team performance continued all the way through the second half.

In the 63rd minute, Vitinha set up Désiré to score again. *3–0!*

Then Khvicha Kvaratskhelia raced onto Ousmane's pass and beat the keeper. *4–0!*

And finally, young sub Senny Mayulu came on, played a clever one-two with Bradley, and completed the rout in style. *5–0!*

What a way to win the Champions League! When the final whistle blew, Gigio collapsed to the floor in his penalty area, crying happy tears this time.

Because they had done it; his PSG team had just made history by becoming Champions of Europe for the first time ever, and every single one of them had played their part.

And also, *he* had done it; yes, at last, after years of trying, Gigio had achieved his childhood dream of winning the Champions League!

Campeones, Campeones, Olé! Olé! Olé!

After collecting his medal, Gigio walked on towards the trophy, where he stopped to share a special hug with Ousmane and Vitinha. Just look at what they'd achieved together – amazing!

As captain, Marquinhos had the honour of lifting the Champions League trophy first, and then one by one, the players all took it in turns to raise it high into the sky.

Hurraaaaaaaay!... Hurraaaaaaaay!

Once everyone had got their hands on the prize, it was time to get the real PSG party started. Gigio posted another three-word message to his followers:

'No. Sleep. Tonight.'

CHAPTER TWENTY

MOVING TO MANCHESTER... CITY!

After playing such an important part in PSG's Champions League win, surely Gigio's position was pretty safe as the club's first-choice keeper? Wrong!

When he asked to discuss a new contract, they couldn't agree on a deal, and when PSG lost 3–0 to Chelsea in July 2025's FIFA Club World Cup final, manager Luis Enrique decided that enough was enough; he wanted a different kind of keeper. Rather than a classic shot-stopper like Gigio, he preferred to have someone who was better at passing, and more comfortable with the ball at his feet.

Someone like Brazilian Renato Marin, who joined

PSG that same month, July 2025…

…or Frenchman Lucas Chevalier, who they signed for €40 million in early August…

Two new keepers! Uh-oh – what did that mean for Gigio's future at the club? He soon found out the answer when he wasn't even selected in the squad for PSG's UEFA Super Cup final against Tottenham.

What?! Really? That was it, then; it was definitely time for him to go…

'To the special Paris fans,' Gigio wrote an emotional letter to the PSG fans he called special. He wrote with pride how he had given everything to earn his place as the team's goalkeeper. He went on to express how sad he was that he was no longer part of the group.

After winning 10 trophies in just four years at the club, Gigio was sorry not to say a proper goodbye to the supporters at the Parc des Princes, but never mind – he had to move on. So, where would he go next?

According to his agent, England looked the most likely destination. They were considering the Premier League as it could be the right place for an important player like Gigio. They were aiming high too: the only Italian to have won the Premier League was Mario Balotelli, and Gigio was determined to become the second.

Interesting! So which title-chasing club would win the race to sign Gigio?

Chelsea, who were thinking about swapping out Robert Sánchez?

Manchester City, who were looking for a long-term replacement for Ederson?

Or Manchester United, who needed someone to take over from André Onana?

By late August, it was down to the two Manchester clubs – so, which one would Gigio choose?

For Gigio, growing up in Italy, United had always been the most famous English club, but after finishing 15th the previous season, were they really ready to challenge for the top trophies again? It didn't seem that way…

And while Gigio loved the idea of working with a world-class manager like Pep Guardiola, would he really suit City's passing style? After all, he was a very different kind of keeper to Ederson! And what about James Trafford? Hadn't they just brought him back to the club to become the new Number 1?

But in the end, all it took was one exciting meeting with Pep, and Gigio's mind was made up: City was where he wanted to go! Now, they just needed to agree a transfer fee with PSG…

A deal was finally done for £26 million on transfer deadline day, and City were ready to announce their big new signing: 'We're delighted to confirm the arrival of Gianluigi Donnarumma!'

Gigio was so proud to have signed for Manchester City. He was joining a squad with world-class talent, led by one of the greatest football managers, Pep Guardiola. This was a club any player would be proud to join.

What shirt number had Gigio chosen to wear this time? Well, with '99' unavailable and '1' already taken by James, Gigio went for '25', the date of his AC Milan first-team debut way back in October 2015, plus his birthday *and* his partner Alessia's birthday.

With all that sorted, it was time to get to work!

Gigio was really looking forward to a fresh start and a new challenge, but unfortunately, there would be no pre-season period to help him settle in and get up to speed. The 2025–26 Premier League season had already started, and next up for City was a massive Manchester derby against United!

CHAPTER TWENTY-ONE

DEBUT IN THE DERBY

14 September 2025, Etihad Stadium, Manchester

On transfer deadline day, both Manchester clubs had signed new goalkeepers, but would either of them make their debut in the local derby? In the end, United manager Ruben Amorim decided to leave Senne Lammens on the bench for the big game, but which City keeper would Pep choose to play: James or Gigio?

The answer rang out loudly around the Etihad Stadium before kick-off: 'Number 25: Gianluigi DONNARUMMA!'

Hurraaaaaaaay!

Making his City debut in the Manchester derby? No big deal! Gigio was far too experienced to get nervous about something like that. After all, he had played in a Euro final for Italy, plus a Champions League final for PSG, and he'd won both of them…

'Good luck!' Rodri said once the players were out on the pitch, giving his new keeper a pat on the back.

'Thanks,' Gigio replied with a calm and confident smile. 'Now let's go and WIN!'

In only the fourth minute of the match, United's new striker Benjamin Šeško turned on the edge of the City box and took a shot at goal, but diving to his right, Gigio was able to reach out and make a comfortable stop.

Hurraaaaaaaay!

Good – Gigio was off to a saving start, and soon City were winning too, thanks to a header from Phil Foden. After that, their new keeper didn't have much to do for the rest of the first half, but everything he did, Gigio did to the best of his ability:

Catching a curling free kick from Bruno Fernandes…

Punching away crosses…

Coming out to collect loose balls…

Launching counterattacks with accurate throws…

Firing long kicks towards Erling Haaland and Jérémy Doku up front…

Playing short passes to defenders Rúben Dias and Joško Gvardiol…

Great work, Gigio!

Early in the second half, Erling raced through to score a second goal for City. Was that it – game over already?

But even though most of the action was going on at the other end of the pitch, Gigio knew that he couldn't switch off for a second. He had to keep his mind in the present, in the moment. The score was still only 2–0, anything could happen, and as a keeper, it was his job to be ready for anything…

As Patrick Dorgu's deep cross floated across the City box, it didn't look too dangerous, but when it dropped to Bryan Mbeumo at the back post, he struck the ball sweetly on the volley, sending it flying towards the bottom corner…

In a flash, Gigio threw his body down and his long right arm out to push the ball past the post. *SAVED! Hurraaaaaaaay!*

'You hero!' Ruben roared, running over to hug his keeper, and he was followed by Rodri, Joško, and then Nico O'Reilly, who all gave Gigio high-fives. How lucky they were to have such a safe pair of gloves in goal!

That magical save turned out to be a key moment in the match. Just seven minutes later, Erling went up the other end and scored again to secure a crucial victory for City.

'YESSSSSSSSSS!' Gigio punched the air as the final whistle blew. A 3–0 win in the Derby *and* a clean sheet – what a dream debut!

Walking around the pitch afterwards, Gigio felt like the most popular person in the world because everyone wanted to hug him and say well done, including his manager.

'Hey – that save in the second half?' Pep said with a wide smile. 'Incredible! It's great to have you here.'

Thanks, Boss! In the end, it was Erling who won

the Player of the Match award, but as he collected his prize, he made sure to praise his new teammate, believing the title could have gone to Donnarumma for his unbelievable performance.

Cheers, mate! Gigio had only been at City for two weeks, but the other players had made him feel so welcome that it already seemed like home.

From Castellammare di Stabia to Milan, to Paris, to Manchester – Gigio's fantastic football journey had taken him all over Europe and all the way to the top, with both club and country. At the age of 26, he had already achieved so much, and there would be plenty more big, exciting moments to come:

A new Champions League adventure with City…

A thrilling Premier League title race…

And hopefully, a trip to the 2026 World Cup with Italy too.

'Bring it on!' Gigio thought to himself, with the calm confidence of a superstar keeper.

AC Milan

🏆 Supercoppa Italiana: 2016

PSG

🏆 Ligue 1: 2021–22, 2022–23, 2023–24, 2024–25
🏆 Coupe de France: 2023–24, 2024–25
🏆 Trophée des Champions: 2022, 2023, 2024
🏆 UEFA Champions League: 2024–25

Italy

🏆 Euro 2020

Individual

🏆 Italian Golden Boy Award: 2019

🏆 Serie A Goalkeeper of the Year: 2019–20, 2020–21

🏆 Euros Player of the Tournament: 2020

🏆 Euros Team of the Tournament: 2020

🏆 Yashin Trophy: 2021, 2025

🏆 UNFP Ligue 1 Goalkeeper of the Year: 2021–22, 2023–24

🏆 UEFA Champions League Team of the Season: 2024–25

🏆 Premier League Save of the Month: September 2025

DONNARUMMA

25 · THE FACTS

NAME: Gianluigi Donnarumma

DATE OF BIRTH: 25 February 1999

PLACE OF BIRTH: Castellammare di Stabia

Age: 26

NATIONALITY: Italian

BEST FRIENDS: his brother Antonio, and Manuel Locatelli

CURRENT CLUB: Manchester City

POSITION: GK

THE STATS

Height (cm):	196
Club appearances:	429
Club goals:	0
Club trophies:	11
International appearances:	79
International goals:	0
International trophies:	1
BALLON D'ORS:	0

 ★ ★ ★ **HERO RATING: 88** ★ ★ ★ 

GREATEST MOMENTS

After months of watching on from the subs bench, this was the day Gigio finally made his first-team debut for AC Milan, while also becoming the youngest keeper ever to start a Serie A match. Sadly, he couldn't quite keep a clean sheet on this occasion, but his team won, and Gigio was soon their first choice in goal…

23 DECEMBER 2016, JUVENTUS 1–1 AC MILAN (MILAN WON 4–3 ON PENALTIES)

In this Supercoppa Italiana final, Gigio was up against his childhood hero Gigi Buffon. When the match went all the way to penalties, only one of them could be the hero, but which incredible Italian keeper would it be? It would be Gigio! With a save to deny Paulo Dybala, he won the shoot-out, securing his first and only trophy for AC Milan. It was also the start of Gigio the Spot-kick King…

11 JULY 2021, ITALY 1–1 ENGLAND (ITALY WON 3–2 ON PENALTIES)

As Euro 2020 progressed, Gigio just got better and better, but his best performance came in the big one: the final against England at Wembley. From 1–0 down, Italy fought back to draw 1–1. Then, for the second time at the tournament, Gigio stood tall and became their shoot-out hero. After saving penalties from Jadon Sancho and Bukayo Saka, it was all over and Italy were the new European Champions!

31 MAY 2025, PSG 5–0 INTER MILAN

Gigio's best performances actually came earlier in the competition, against Liverpool and Arsenal, but this was the amazing night when both he and his club PSG finally won the Champions League for the first time. And what a way to win it, by thrashing AC Milan's local rivals Inter 5–0! Together, Gigio and his incredible teammates had just made history.

14 SEPTEMBER 2025, MANCHESTER CITY 3–0 MANCHESTER UNITED

Making his City debut in the Manchester derby, fearless Gigio was ready to become an instant club hero. He didn't have lots to do as City dominated the game, but when his new team needed him, he was there, diving across his goal to keep out Bryan Mbuemo's volley. That was later voted Premier League Save of the Month – what a dream start for Gigio!

TEST YOUR KNOWLEDGE

QUESTIONS

1. Growing up, what position did Gigio's brother Antonio play on the football pitch?

2. Aged seven, Gigio watched his country Italy win which major international football tournament?

3. How old was Gigio when he left home to move to the AC Milan academy?

4. How old was Gigio when he made his first-team debut for AC Milan?

5. Which shirt number did Gigio always wear at AC Milan, and why?

6. How many penalties did Gigio save for Italy at Euro 2020?

7. True or false – Gigio was named Player of the Tournament at Euro 2020?

8. When he first arrived at PSG, Gigio had to compete with which other world-class keeper?

9. At Euro 2024, Gigio saved a penalty from which midfield maestro?

10. Who was the PSG captain when they won the Champions League in 2025?

11. Which shirt number did Gigio pick at Manchester City, and why? (There are lots of reasons)

1. He was a goalkeeper, just like him! 2. The 2006 World Cup 3. Fourteen 4. 14 5. 99 – because 1999 was the year he was born 6. Three – 1 against Spain, then 2 against England 7. True! He became the first goalkeeper to ever win the award. 8. Keylor Navas 9. Croatia's Luka Modrić 10. Marquinhos 11. Number 25 – because: a) 99 wasn't allowed, b) James Trafford already had Number 1, c) 25 was the date when he made his AC Milan debut way back in October 2015, d) his birthday is on the 25th, and e) his partner Alessia's birthday is also on the 25th.

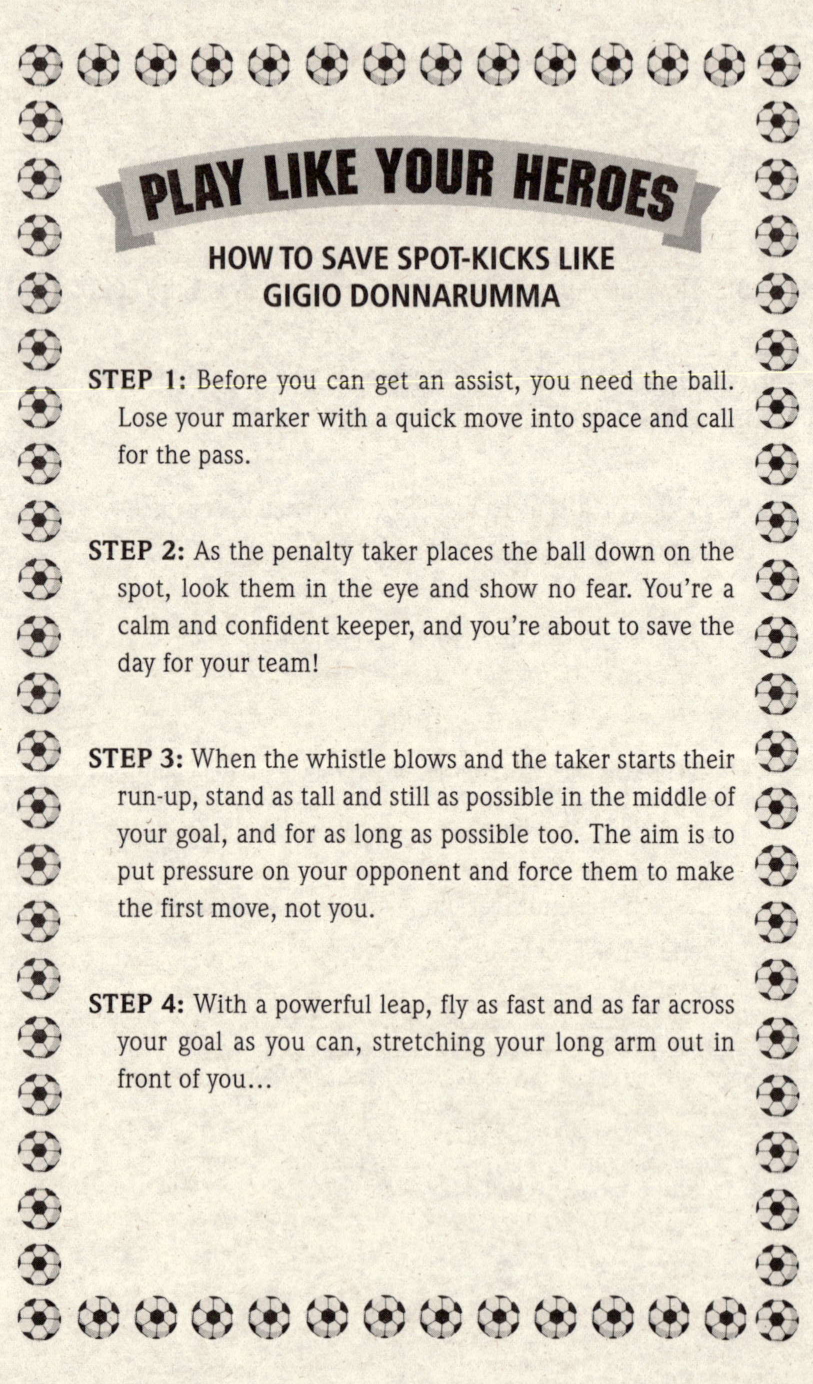

PLAY LIKE YOUR HEROES

HOW TO SAVE SPOT-KICKS LIKE GIGIO DONNARUMMA

STEP 1: Before you can get an assist, you need the ball. Lose your marker with a quick move into space and call for the pass.

STEP 2: As the penalty taker places the ball down on the spot, look them in the eye and show no fear. You're a calm and confident keeper, and you're about to save the day for your team!

STEP 3: When the whistle blows and the taker starts their run-up, stand as tall and still as possible in the middle of your goal, and for as long as possible too. The aim is to put pressure on your opponent and force them to make the first move, not you.

STEP 4: With a powerful leap, fly as fast and as far across your goal as you can, stretching your long arm out in front of you…

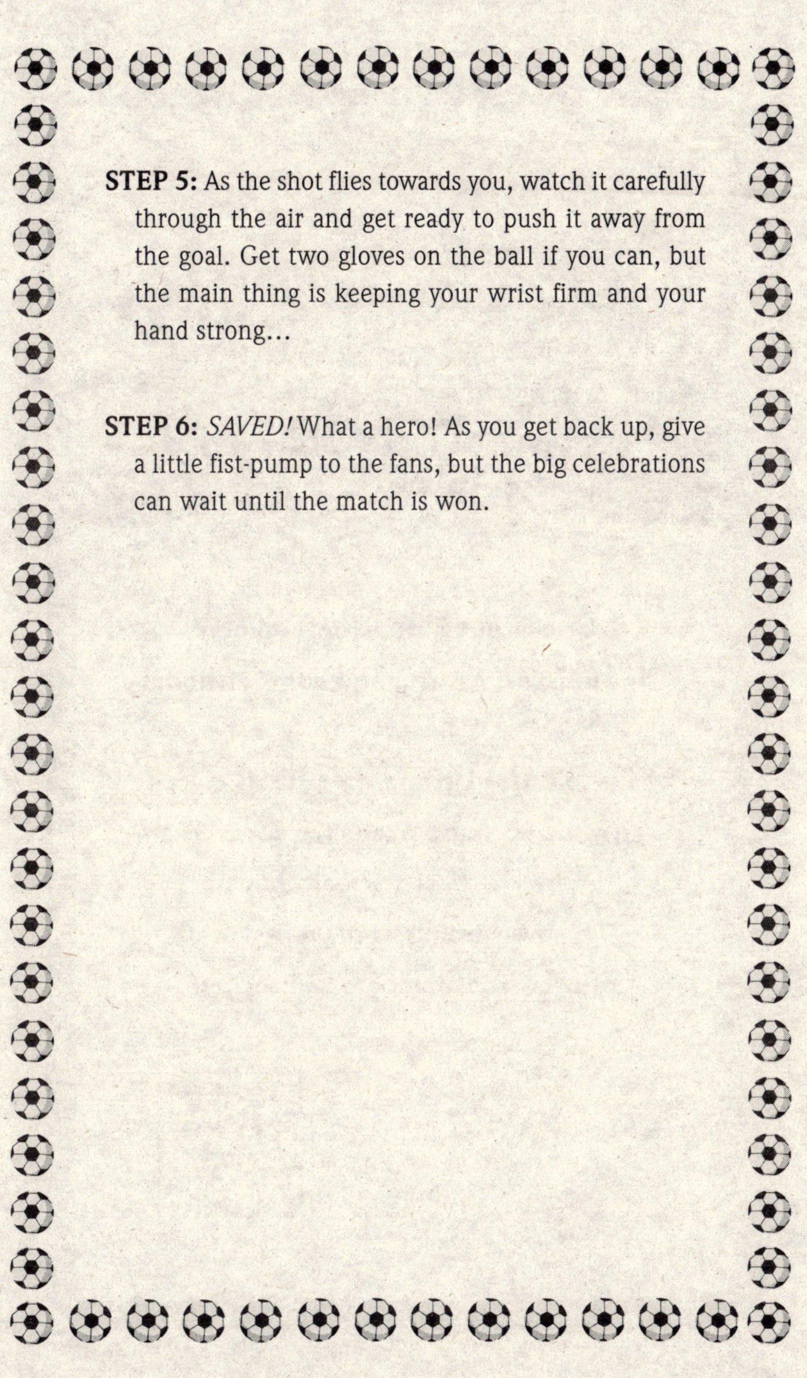

STEP 5: As the shot flies towards you, watch it carefully through the air and get ready to push it away from the goal. Get two gloves on the ball if you can, but the main thing is keeping your wrist firm and your hand strong…

STEP 6: *SAVED!* What a hero! As you get back up, give a little fist-pump to the fans, but the big celebrations can wait until the match is won.

Check out heroesfootball.com
for quizzes, games, and competitions!

Plus join the Ultimate Football Heroes
Fan Club to score exclusive content and
be the first to hear about
new books and events.
heroesfootball.com/subscribe/